Der Fingerhüter.

Der Tugend starcker Schutz, bezwingt der Laster Trutz.

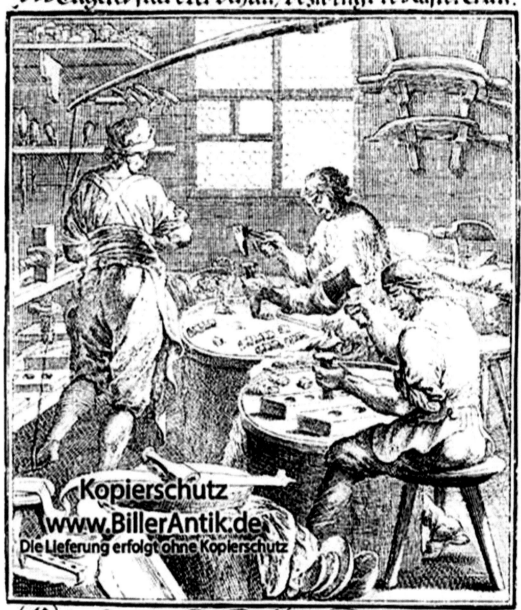

Gedult ist wie ein Fingerhut,
steckt unter diesem Herz und Muth,
so stechen keine Laster-Nadeln,
die der Verleumder Bossheit weist,
dann dieser Spitze bricht zuletzt.
Wan Lob und Ruhm die Unschuld adeln.

Metal Sewing-Thimbles Found in Britain

Brian Read

principal illustrator

Mike Trevarthen

ARCHAEOPRESS ARCHAEOLOGY

ARCHAEOPRESS PUBLISHING LTD
Summertown Pavilion
18-24 Middle Way
Summertown
Oxford OX2 7LG

www.archaeopress.com

ISBN 978 1 78491 945 0
ISBN 978 1 78491 946 7 (e-Pdf)

© Archaeopress and B Read 2018

Frontispiece: Der Fingerhüter (Christoph Weigel 1698). A Nuremberg thimble-maker's workshop

Printed in England by Holywell Press, Oxford

For Val, for her support and encouragement

Contents

List of Figures

Notes on Illustrations

The principal illustrator *et al* skilfully produced accurate representations of actual thimbles catalogued herein though some were drawn from photographs that frequently failed to show all perspectives or detail, particularly plan views. Catalogue drawings are approximately actual size with the exception of detail, which is enlarged. Maximum metric dimensions for all objects are noted within the text: dimensions for squashed items may be slightly larger than when intact. Copyright acknowledgements and Treasure, PAS, UKDFD and museum accession numbers are also included in the text. Thimbles and other objects shown in Figs are not to scale and except for Fig. 3, come from British depositions, primarily detectorists' finds and some archaeological.

Drawings Nos 1-6, 8-18, 20, 22, 24-60, 62-82, 84-88, 90-105, 107-116, 118-119, 122-124, 126-140, 142-149, 151-170, 172, 174-180, 182-184, 186, 189-220, 222-233, 237-243, 245-248, 251, 254-258, 261-264, 266-283, 285-291, 294-308, 314 copyright © Mike Trevarthen; Nos 39-313, 315-322 copyright © Patrick Read; No. 315 copyright © Claire Goodey; Nos 7, 19, 21, 23, 61, 83, 89, 106, 117, 120-121, 125, 141, 150, 168, 171, 173, 181, 185, 187-189, 221, 234-236, 244, 249-250, 252-253, 259-260, 264, 284, 292-293 copyright © Nick Griffiths; enlarged makers' marks Nos 254-255, 271 copyright © Tom Redmayne; Fig. 3 photo copyright © and reproduced courtesy of 'American School of Classical Studies at Athens, Corinth Excavations'; Fig. 4 photo copyright © and reproduced courtesy of the MoL; Figs 8, 30 copyright © Lewis Murray and reproduced courtesy of Shetland Museum and Archive; Figs 19, 21-24 reproduced courtesy of the City Library of Nuremberg; Fig. 35 copyright © and reproduced courtesy of Nigel Mills and Greenlight Publishing; Fig. 37 copyright © and reproduced courtesy of the Rijksdienst voor Cultureel Erfgoed, the Netherlands; Fig. 39 copyright © and courtesy of Penlee House and Gallery Museum, Penzance; Fig. 41 copyright © and reproduced courtesy of the PAS. Reproduction of any illustration is prohibited without express permission in writing from the respective copyright owner.

Abbreviations

B – base

D – diameter

H – height

L – length

T – thickness

 W – width

No. Nos – number / numbers

acc. – accession number

cat. – catalogue number

ill. – illustration number

Fig. / Figs – Figure / Figures

PAS – Portable Antiquities Scheme

MoL – Museum of London

SM – Salisbury Museum

UKDFD – United Kingdom Detecting Finds' Database

V&A – Victoria & Albert Museum

WHM – Wiltshire Heritage Museum

MDC – Metal-Detecting Club

Acknowledgements

This study would have been impossible without the generous assistance of many people and institutions. My gratitude is extended to the landowners who permit searches of their respective holdings, independent metal-detectorists (hereafter detectorists) and members of MDCs who allowed their finds to be recorded, and individuals who assisted in other ways. But for them this diversity of metal sewing-thimbles, finger-guards and palm-irons would remain unfound and unrecorded.

Firstly: Alan Ausden, John Baker, Richard Berry, Prof. R A Booth, Gary Crace, Dean Crawford, Alun Crichton, Patrick Donnelly, Peter Faxholm, Tony Hale, Steve Healey, Andrea Herbert, Ian Hennwinkle, E T James, Paul Lancaster, David Lange, Simon Law, Peter Leech, Tom Lynch, Kati Manning, Paul Manning, Sharon McKee, Tony Mead, Anthony Mims, Jeremy de Montfalcon, Richard Otterbeck, Maggie Packer, John Packer, Michael Page, Keith Palmer, Christopher Phillips, Brian Poole, Clive Rasdall, Patrick Read, Tom Redmayne, Chris Roberts, John Ruczynski, Mike Ruczynski, Liz Tyler, James Ward, Chris Welch, Will Weller and Simon Wildman; Bloxwich Research Society – Bob Gumbley; Brighton and District MDC – Dave Smith; Cardiff Scan Club – Patrick Good; Cotswold Heritage and Detecting Society – Steve Taylor; Derby Artefacts Recovery Club – Lisa Grace and Adam Staples; Detecting Wales – Mike Mceabe, Martin Merriman, Paul Merriman, Mike Taylor and Neil Woollacott; Dorchester MDC – David Layton; East Devon MDC – Mike Applegate, Jim Autton, Jon Chapman, Ron Gibson, Graham Smith, George Stevens, Steve Thomas, Nigel Tucker, Rick Ward, Trevor Ward, Sam Weller, Winn Weller, Richard Wells, Paul Wood and John Wright; Grantham Search Club – Steve Critchley; Gwent MDC – Dave Allen; Isle of Wight MDC – Dave Dent, Shane Downer, Brian Hawkes, John Jerram and Mick Rugg; Lincolnshire Historical Search Society MDC – Patrick Filgate; Mid Cornwall History Hunters – Vic Chapman; Northamptonshire Artefact Recovery Club – Tony Smithurst; Norwich Detectors – Ron Morley; Oxford Blues MDC – Dai Devonald; Romney Marshland MDC – Phil Castle and Dave Hannon; Society of Thames Mudlarks – Ken Bellringer, John Higginbotham, John Mills, Mark Smalley, Andy Johannesen and Ian Smith; Stour Valley Search and Recovery Club – Dave Eagles and Bob Tydeman; Thames and Field MDC – Steven Camp; Torbay MD Club – Fred Brown and John Parnell; Trowbridge MDC – Ivy Macfarlane; Weekend Wanderers MDC – Colin Silk; Weald and Downland MDC – Tony Brown; Weymouth and Portland MDC – Mike Apps, Jeff Braithwaite, Nigel Bridges, Dave Cobb, Carlos Camposano, Richard Cotton, Alan Davies, Joe Dillon, Mark Ellard, Margaret Hamilton, Ron Howse, Alan Maidment, M Murphy, Carl Walmsley and Jim Walmsley; Yeovil MDC – Mark Cowan, Ian James, Graham Libbey, Robert Lovett, Val MacRae, Paul Miller, Mike Otterbeck, Stephen Simpson, Gordon Sinfield and Hugh Vincent; and those whom desire anonymity. Secondly: Archaeological Small Finds – Jörn Schuster; American School of Classical Studies, Athens – Dr Ioulia Tzonou-Herbst and Katherine Petrole MA Museum Studies; Clarks Shoe Museum, Street – Charlotte Berry; De Gratia Coins – Dave Shelley and Gary Croucher; Littlehampton Museum – Jonathan Parrett; Mary Rose Museum, Portsmouth – Stacy Court, Peter Crossman and Sue Judge; Museum of English Rural Life, Reading – Felicity McWilliams; Museum of Knots and Sailors' Ropework, Ipswich – Des Pawson MBE; Museum I22I20I18I Kühnertsgasse, Nuremberg – Dr Inge Lauterbach; Museum of London – Dr Geoff Egan (Specialist Services), Catherine Maloney and Dan Nesbitt (London Archaeological Archive Research Centre) and Nicola Powell (Archaeology); Museum of the Royal Navy, Portsmouth – Richard Noyce (Artefacts); National Maritime Museum, Greenwich – Katy Barrett (Curator of Art), Sarah Kmosena (Collections Store Manager) and Barbara Tomlinson (Artefacts); Netherlands Patent Office – C H Visser; Netherlands National Archive – Nicole Brandt and H Yavuz; Northampton Shoe Museum – Victoria Davies; Nuremberg City Library – Dr Astrid Anhalt and Dr Christine Sauer; Oxfordshire Museum Service – Samantha van de Greer; Pittards Leather PLC, Yeovil – M Dodd; Penlee House and Gallery Museum, Penzance – Katie Herbert; PAS – Frank Basford, Laura Burnett, Julie Cassidy, Garry Crace, Erica Darch, Adam Daubney, Amy Downes, Rebecca Griffiths, Richard Henry, Katie Hinds, Jennifer Jackson, Wendy Scott, Kate Sumnall, Ciorstaidh Hayward Trevarthen, Anna Tyacke, David Williams, Edwin Wood and Danielle Wootton; Rijksmusem van Oudheden – Annemarike Willemsen (curator Medieval Department); Salisbury Museum – Adrian Green; Shetland Museum and Archive – Laurie Goodlad, Jenny Murray (Curator of Collections), Lewis Murray and Helen Whitham; The Tudor Tailor – Dr Jane Malcolm-Davies; University Museum of Zoology, Cambridge – Richard Preece, Curator of Molluscs; University of Newcastle upon Tyne, The Robinson Library – Christine Stevens; Victoria and Albert Museum, London – Susan North; Walsall Leather Museum – David Mills; Western Australian Museum, Shipwreck Galleries – Myra Stanbury; Wiltshire Heritage Museum – Lisa Brown, David Dawson and Kerry Nickels; Searcher Publications – Harry Bain; Somerset County Library Service – Mel Close, Sally Foyne and Sue Wright; UKDFD – Rod Blunt;

Viking Ship Museum, Roskilde, Denmark – Jørn Bohimann. For translating Dutch and German text into English, Edward Cumming, Laurina Deacon and Gert Gesink; Greenlight Publishing – Alan Golbourn, and Nigel Mills for authorising the redrawing and publishing of objects in *Medieval Artefacts* 1999; master goldsmith Barry Sherlock for invaluable technical advice concerning the construction and decoration of metal thimbles and Philippa Foster for the initial cover design, subsequently not used. Line-drawings are the strong-point of this study, all entirely due to the artistic skill of archaeological illustrators Claire Goodey, Nick Griffiths, my son Patrick, and especially Michael Trevarthen (with additional input by Tom Redmayne) – my thanks to them all. Lastly, I am indebted to Nicola Powell for penning the foreword. Any errors remaining are solely the responsibility of the present writer.

Brian Read, Huish Episcopi, Somerset, 2017.

Foreword

Brian Read has been at the forefront of the publication of accessible books for metal detectorists and finds researchers since his first book *History Beneath Our Feet* was published in 1988. This new volume follows on the success of his 2005 *Metal Buttons* and *Hooked Clasps and Eyes*, published in 2009, in which he researched and catalogued specific categories of finds. The late great Geoff Egan wrote the foreword for both books so I am honoured to have been asked to contribute to Brian's new book, *Metal Sewing-Thimbles Found In Britain*. Thimbles are a relatively common find on urban sites, as any of Geoff's published works on London finds show us, and as stray finds in rural locations, though they can often be dismissed beyond simple form and metal by those immune to the charms of these intimate, widely varied objects.

This important book celebrates the humble sewing-thimble, and looks at the varied forms and types of hand protection used when pushing needles through textile and leather from the 13th century up to the early 20th century. He uses data from the Portable Antiquities Scheme and UK Detector Finds Database, as well as those found during controlled archaeological excavation and mudlarking. It is richly enhanced with photographs and drawings, emphasising that no two of these objects are the same, and providing an invaluable resource for detectorists, archaeologists, finds specialists, dress historians, curators and collectors to identify and date types found in Britain. Indeed, this book is likely to reach further, providing comparanda for finds from important sites such as Jamestown, a place that was close to Geoff Egan's heart.

This book cannot be definitive, as new and different thimbles are regularly appearing. This only goes to emphasise the importance of recording each thimble found, however it may be recovered. As ever, close cooperation between archaeology and detecting remains essential in furthering our knowledge of small metal material culture. *Metal Sewing-Thimbles Found In Britain* adds to and builds on the corpus of collected works such as Bridget McConnel's *The Letts Guide to Collecting Thimbles* 1990, the late Edwin Holmes' *A History of Thimbles* 1985, and Magdalina and William Isbister's *More About* volumes as well as the catalogues of stratigraphically recovered finds by Geoff Egan.

The wide variety of thimbles found reflects the equally wide variety of people who would have used them. A thimble can provide us with a wealth of information about its creation, use and ultimate loss. And who can resist putting this most personal of finds onto a little finger, sparing a thought for the maker and the owner as it bears witness to the past?

Nicola Powell (Buckinghamshire, 2017)

Metal Sewing-Thimbles

Introduction

The name *sewing-thimble/s* differentiates these tools from metal thimbles used in specialist occupations, e.g. thatching, threshing, surgery, firearms, ropework or rigging *et al*; and it describes those without a crown or having a closed or partially open crown, but all for propelling needles through textile or leather. Out of their normal working environment, certain specialist metal-thimbles may be mistaken for sewing-thimbles, therefore some catalogued here as the latter are perhaps the former. In this study, for textual brevity, the common description *thimble/s* is used.

The present writer emphasises this work is not definitive, and opinions are based solely on his own physical examination of numerous metal thimbles found in Britain, combined with researching the available archive of primary and secondary publications. Some of the latter, it is fair to say, are frustratingly ambiguous and inconsistent and virtually verbatim of someone else's work, therefore when studying these, circumspection is wise. However, the primary sources are mostly reliable but since their respective publication fresh evidence has inevitably projected new light on the subject.

For dating typical late medieval and early post-medieval metal thimbles of the kinds regularly excavated in Britain, much of the more trustworthy evidence is found in the following literature: On Early Thimbles: A Seventh-Century-AD Example from Punta Secca, Sicily in Context by R J A Wilson *Oxford Journal of Archaeology Vol. 35, Issue 4.* 2016; *Vingeeerhoedoen en naairingen uit de Amsterdamse bodem: Productietechnieken vanaf de Late Middeleeuwen* 1999 by Catherine A Langedijk and Herman F Boon; *The Medieval Household Daily Living c.1150-c.1450* 1998 and *Material Culture in London in an Age of Transition Tudor and Stuart Period Finds c.1450-c.1700 from Excavations at Riverside Sites in Southwark* 2005 each by Dr Geoff Egan; *The Venetian Shipwreck at Gnalić* 2004 edited by Zrinka Mileusnic; *De Vingerhoed in Het Kunstambacht* 1992 by Adrrienne De Smet; *Nuremberg Thimble-makers* 1986 by Helmut Greif; *Nürnberger Fingerhüte* 2014 by Michaela Eigmüller and Inge Lauterbach. Wider information about thimbles made of any material and from any period is found in two invaluable reference books – the late Edwin Holmes *A History of Thimbles* 1985, and Bridget McConnel's *The Letts Guide to Collecting Thimbles* 1991. Unquestionably, Holmes' research forms the benchmark in knowledge about the subject. Magdalena and William Isbister are the current vanguard into research concerning thimbles generally, especially those of metal, and their books and papers listed in the bibliography are essential reading. Des Pawson MBE discusses sailmakers' palm-irons in his commendable Monograph 8 *Sailmakers' Palms* 2010 and *Sailmakers' Palms expanded edition* 2018. The present writer has drawn heavily on the aforesaid works. Also considered are the bibliographical publications listed herein, and *Treasure Hunting* and *The Searcher* magazines. Invaluable information concerning metal thimbles primarily found by detectorists is available on the respective databases of the PAS and UKDFD.

Herein, only metal thimbles (including finger-guards and palm-irons), i.e. copper-alloy, iron/steel, pewter, gold or silver, found in Britain are studied, many of which belong to ubiquitous types while others are unusual or perhaps even rare (notwithstanding, comment is made about certain lead or stone implements of unclear function). Holmes 1985 indicates that pewter was not generally used for making practical thimbles, and mentions several recovered from a 1700-50 context (whether archaeologically or River Thames foreshore reliable, he does not say), and their small size suggests they were children's tokens for games. This present study revealed only a trio of pewter domed thimbles: a crushed example from the River Thames foreshore, London, one so tiny it is perhaps a child's toy, and another large enough to be functional. Apart from one here, thimbles earlier than the 19th century and made of gold do not seem to feature in the known record as detecting or archaeological finds. Emphasis is given to the constructional processes of metal thimbles, of the types covered, and how these methods often created features that may aid reasonably accurate dating. For an accepted understanding of how and when certain late medieval and post-medieval copper-alloy thimbles were made, one cannot do better than to study the aforesaid work by Langedijk and Boon 1999.

Detectorists, including members of the Society of Thames Mudlarks, are responsible for finding in Britain most of the metal thimbles, finger-guards and palm-irons in this present assemblage, and the former span from possibly the 12th century through to the early 19th while the latter two are seemingly post-medieval. Notable absentees are 18th-century silver filigree domed thimbles, with not one example in the known detecting record. The 19th and 20th centuries saw an explosion in the types and styles of metal domed thimbles and, all being easily recognisable, are largely omitted from this present study. Findspots are denoted in italics: to protect the confidentiality of landowners and sites, the omission of precise provenance details is deliberate.

Essentially, four forms of stone, organic or metal tool to propel a needle through textile or leather are recognised:

- ring-type thimble – aka tailor's thimble, sewing-ring, thimble-ring
- domed thimble
- open-top thimble
- palm-iron – aka pusher, palm-guard pusher

An understanding of the evolution of the English word 'thimble' is best explained by Holmes 1985, who quotes a verse from a 12th-century Arabic poem entitled 'The Thimble' composed by Al-Liss, a Moor from Seville:

'Tis like a helmet, nicked
Where thrusting lances pricked;
Some sword has dispossessed
The helmet of its crest'.

The poem, which is the earliest written reference concerning thimbles, accurately describes the early medieval inordinately large, distinctive cast copper-alloy domed thimbles made in Cordoba, Spain (see below) seemingly modelled on the Moorish military helmet. Holmes continues, Al-Liss used the arabicized Persian word *kustubān* meaning thumb guard; which in true Persian is *angushtvān* meaning finger protector, a word found in archery publications. In India the word is *angushtāneh*, Bengali *angushtāna* and Hindi *anghootyum*. The English word thimble evolved from the Old English (Old Saxon) *thūma*, meaning 'thumb', which provides the derivation 'thymel'. Sometime during the 15th century the letter b was added giving us 'thimble', from the Middle English word 'tho(u)mbe'. This does not imply thimbles were necessarily worn on the thumb. Even earlier, the German words for thimble and ring-type thimble are *fingerhüt* and *nähring* respectively, and in Dutch, *vingerhoed* and *naairing*.

Thimbles of any type and material are unknown from ancient Egypt or Greece respectively, and the first trustworthy tangible evidence for metal thimbles comes from China during the Warring States Period (475-221 BC) (Wilson 2016 *et al*). Written mentions of Roman thimbles are: H S Cuming 1879 '... ring-type thimbles were discovered in Herculaneum'; Sylvia Groves 1966 '... bronze thimbles had been found at Pompeii and Herculaneum', and Helmut Greif 1984 'Pompeii and Herculaneum ... buried by Vesuvias ... metal thimbles must have been in use about 2000 years ago' (Greif also describes Roman thimbles). Notwithstanding, Holmes 1985 indicates there is not any archaeological stratified evidence for thimbles of any material or type from any Roman site, including Pompeii or Herculaneum. Holmes' research is generally accepted as reliable, however, so-called Roman copper-alloy thimbles persist within the museum, archaeological and metal-detecting fraternities. Interestingly, in 1988 a (?) cast copper-alloy ring-type thimble came from a c.AD 100-125 archaeological stratified context in Ephesus, Turkey (Wilson 2016). Despite this thimble being the earliest recorded from a Roman stratified context anywhere in the Roman Empire, it's speculative whether it is truly Roman: Wilson 2016 indicates it is a possible Far Eastern import, perhaps accompanying silk yarn and fine steel needles arriving from China. Whether or not the great Roman civilisation did use metal thimbles is a debate that will rumble on until an example is recovered from an archaeological stratified Roman context in Britain or elsewhere.

Said to be the earliest evidence for copper-alloy ring-type thimbles, about 100, in Europe is from archaeologically stratified 9th- – 12th-century deposits in Byzantine Corinth, Greece (Davidson G. R. 1952), though Wilson 2016 challenges this statement, saying their contexts were unstratified. However, nine ring-types have been found at various Eastern Mediterranean locations, all archaeologically secure 7th- century contexts: the earliest from a c.AD 600-625 stratified context in Punta Secca, Sicily (Wilson 2016). The Punta Secca discovery nullifies the Corinth ring-types.

Copper-alloy ring-type thimbles were seemingly current in 12th-century Germany (Holmes 1985) and an early 13th-century archaeologically stratified context in Amsterdam revealed a fragmented example (Langedijk and Boon 1999, ill. 34, cat. 292). Where these early ring-type thimbles originated is unclear, but they were perhaps cast, a technique that continued for both ring-types and domed until the advent of hammering which Langedijk and Boon 1999 say started in the mid-15th century. Archaeological evidence from London refutes this date – hammered domed thimbles were produced from at least the 14th century (see below). Interestingly, the Punta Secca ring-type thimble, the incomplete one from Amsterdam, the Eastern Mediterranean examples including those found in Corinth are all remarkably similar to late medieval ring-types recovered from British soil. This begs the question – do some British-found examples warrant a much earlier attribution? Isbister 2001, when describing children's thimbles, wrote, 'the earliest [a ring-type] ... found near Salisbury ... probably dates to the 12th or 13th century'. Regrettably, supporting evidence for this statement is not provided, however, the present writer believes it may be correct.

From at least 1350, and throughout the 15th and 16th centuries, Nuremberg was Europe's primary producer of copper-alloy thimbles, and their manufacture there, albeit decreasingly, continued until the end of the 18th century. The Netherlands eventually overtook Nuremberg and predominated until the end of the 17th century. Thimble manufactories were also operating in France at least by the 13th century, and at similar times in different areas of Germany, Wallonia in Belgium and other European centres but in Britain large-scale commercial copper-ally thimble production did not start until the late 17th century (see John Lofting, below), albeit artisan thimble-makers worked here from at least c.1650. Britain's needs were supplied from mainland Europe, e.g. between 29 December 1682 and 1 February 1683 19,500 thimbles were imported into London, and 304,000 between March and June 1692 (Houghton 1727/28), without doubt these came from the Netherlands. Determining the age of some metal thimbles found in unstratified contexts, or where they were made, is problematic, therefore it is wise to be circumspect – for many described in this present study, dating and/or provenance is tentative.

Medieval and post-medieval thimbles primarily were made from copper or an alloy of: scientific analysis is the only way to determine a precise composition therefore it is sensible to describe this metal as copper alloy, albeit thimble-collectors usually say 'brass'. Iron, silver or gold thimbles were no doubt current in Britain during the later Middle Ages too, though sumptuary law would have restricted those made of precious metal to royalty and the nobility. No medieval silver thimbles of any type were noted during this study. In the early 16th century silver became more plentiful and thimbles (and other trinkets, too) were made from this metal, however, until it was repealed in 1604, again sumptuary law ensured that only people above a certain rank were allowed to own them. Apart from four early post-medieval silver domed-thimbles here, this perhaps explains the apparent absence of silver thimbles in archaeological contexts and as detecting or Thames Mudlarks' discoveries. Paradoxically, Holmes 1985 indicates their widespread use, however, the lack of conclusive evidence from the soil suggests otherwise.

Ring-type thimbles are simply virtual tubes, or barrel-shaped or truncated cones of metal, open at both ends – one end of which or the widest end fits over the finger – and these may be cast, hammered sheet, sheet with longitudinal soldered seams or sheet with longitudinal unsoldered seams. Soldered and unsoldered seams may be butted, scarfed or both lapped and scarfed.

Thimbles with closed rounded, flat or pointed crowns are best described as domed, the basic construction of which, depending on period, is either cast one-piece, hammered sheet one-piece, or composite two, three- or six-piece sheet with longitudinal (sides) and horizontal (crowns to sides) soldered seams. Dated at c.12th – c.15th century, a Hispano-Moresque large cast copper-alloy domed thimble here is possibly the known record's earliest domed thimble from a British deposition. Composite two-piece domed thimbles with both longitudinal and horizontal soldered seams may have been first made about the mid-15th century, but complete confirmed examples of this date were not noted during this present study, however, evidence for one possibility is discussed below. Longitudinal seams are usually butted and soldered, and horizontal seams either butted or scarfed soldered. As with some ring-types, however, longitudinal soldered seams may be both lapped and scarfed, as noted on several examples in this present assemblage. Sometime during the late 18th century mass composite construction of domed thimbles gave way to the mechanical deep-drawing method (see below); notwithstanding, at this time artisan composite production continued, two practices often responsible for assigning an incorrect age to a thimble. For example, herein, a domed silver composite three-piece thimble could easily be ascribed as 16th or 17th century; however, it is stamped with the international fineness mark 925 thereby confirming it as 19th – 20th century. It was around the late 18th century that steel caps began to be soldered on crowns of some silver or copper-alloy domed thimbles.

A cross between the ring-type and domed thimble has a much larger circular hole in the apex of the crown (see below). These thimbles are seemingly uncommon in Britain and in this present work are classified as 'open-top', of which two styles are noted – both cast copper-alloy – one quite tall and the other somewhat stubbier.

Differentiating cast or hammered thimbles of any type from those having soldered seams is invariably relatively easy. Examination of both the outside and inside, using magnification if necessary, may reveal the telltale lines of solder shown in a different colour. Nonetheless, a skilful artisan would attempt to disguise seams (especially with gold or silver thimbles) by incorporating them into any decoration.

Crowns of certain late medieval one-piece domed thimbles exhibit a small circular hole, though unproven, possibly formed by a pin securing a casting mould core: confusingly, some hammered domed thimbles also feature similar holes. Domed thimbles in this current study revealed that it appears only those with a tonsure (see below) have such a piercing. Also noted on crowns of many cast or composite sheet domed thimbles is a tiny centring pit, and internal turning striations, two or more basal peripheral equidistant notches, and/or a basal wedge inside with oblique grooves outside, all of which suggest being held in a lathe chuck for finishing or knurling (see below).

Both silver and copper-alloy domed and ring-type thimbles were made by hammering, i.e. using different-size punches to force a flan of sheet metal alternately into a series of decreasing-size circular holes in an iron swaging-block. This process is often called 'deep-drawing', a term which really ought to be reserved for mechanical deep drawing. Such thimbles may exhibit creased or split sides caused by insufficient annealing. Domed thimbles lacking any of the aforesaid characteristics can make it difficult to differentiate cast and hammered forms. Size and mass are unreliable guides though cast examples may have thicker sides. Langedijk and Boon 1999 offer an alternative method of hammering, i.e. 'Round metal plates were gradually raised by hammering them on an edge until the shape of a thimble was reached'. This statement is questionable; while raising is a manufacturing technique suitable for larger metalwork, for small items such as thimbles it's impractical (pers. comm. a master goldsmith).

Pits – aka indentations, dimples, holes, blind-holes – were either drilled or punched, and applied in columns (often oblique), concentric circles, left- or right-hand spirals, random or a combination of configurations. Possibly the earliest configuration is columns or concentric circles, as testified by the aforesaid examples from China, Punta Secca and the Eastern Mediterranean. Pits may completely cover the thimble while Holmes 1985 indicates up to c.1650 (a contentious date, see below) many were left with a tonsure-like patch on the crown, the size and shape of which varies, some with and some without a crown hole. Sides of both ring-type and domed thimbles frequently feature circumferential upper and/or basal plain bands that vary in width. Drilled pits are obviously circular while those punched may be circular, oval, D-shaped, reversed D-shaped, square, rectangular, elongated ovoid, triangular, crosses or a variety of star shapes. Many thimbles with triangular pits are said to be French (Isbister 2002/2011); however, Nuremberg thimble-makers also applied this shape, as perhaps did English producers. A mixture of pit shapes on the same thimble is not unusual. The size of pits is an unreliable guide to a thimble's age; it probably only indicates suitability for use with a particular gauge of needle.

Circumferential basal single or double engraved grooves or bands of punched dots are apparent on many medieval domed and ring-type thimbles. Use of such grooves continued into the 17th century. The known record seemingly has only five medieval thimbles – two domed and three open-top – with one or more circumferential engraved grooves separating the pits from the tonsured crown or upper hole. Other decoration on medieval thimbles is uncommon though engraving, die punching, drilling and openwork are known. Pits were occasionally arranged to leave patterns of geometric strapwork or organic motifs, usually but not always outlined with linear engraving, or pits themselves formed geometric or curlicue shapes. White-metal coating, probably tin; gilding or a black coating, perhaps linseed oil (Holmes 1985) (black coating is common on other early and late post-medieval small metalwork), also appeared during the 16th century, while niello is apparently known on thimbles from the mid-15th century to the 18th though other than one mid-17th-century English silver domed thimble, none were noted during this current study. Gilding is occasionally evident on thimbles from the early post-medieval period through to the 19th century.

Excavated medieval and post-medieval domed thimbles with surviving leather, paper, twine, textile or metal internal sleeves are recorded. Presumably such inserts provided comfort and/or a better fit or strength, and evidence is provided that metal sleeves acted as repairs to damaged crowns (see below). A not uncommon discovery, which is easily mistaken for a metal internal sleeve, is a domed thimble with another inserted inside; this possibly represents a convenient method of storing. With regard to excavated domed thimbles retaining organic sleeves, Susan North, dress historian at the V&A Museum, London, provided an opinion based on photos, that inserts on one (see below) are '... coarse, plain-weave fabric ... possibly linen'.

Metal domed thimbles occasionally show obvious evidence of major repair or alteration and these are termed 'hybrid' thimbles (Isbister 2011). One definite hybrid and one possible are included here (see below).

The palm-iron – aka pusher, palm guard – is probably the earliest form of tool to push needles, initially perhaps being a rudimentary piece of stone or organic material cupped in the palm, or held by the fingers. Stone pushers ascribed as *c.*10,000 BC are recorded, and copper-alloy pushers, called *acutrudia*, dating from the 11th to the 15th centuries are known from the Middle East and Turkey (McConnel 1991). Some form of palm-iron is possibly what the Romans used, but paradoxically such tools are absent from the Roman period archaeological record.

In Britain, entirely due to detectorists and Thames Mudlarks, substantial cast metal tools now recognised as seemingly post-medieval palm-irons are becoming more apparent in the known record (see below). Other cast leaden objects invariably described as palm-guards/pushers are frequently found by detectorists though this function is unproven (see below).

Figure 1. Composite three-piece sheet silver domed thimble c.19th – c.20th century. Note longitudinal soldered butt seam and 925 fineness stamp. Private collection.

Figure 2. Hybrid sheet silver domed thimble with a probable replacement flat crown c.19th – c.20th century. *Dorset.*

Metal Ring-Type Thimbles

Ring-type thimbles *c.* early 13th century – *c.*1450

The Punta Secca, Corinth and other Eastern Mediterranean archaeological evidence suggests that in Britain the ring-type is possibly the earliest form of late medieval copper-alloy thimble. The aforesaid archaeologically excavated example in Amsterdam (Langedijk and Boon 1999, ill. 34, cat. 292), is evidence that ring-types were current from at least the early 13th century in northern mainland Europe and possibly in Britain too.

Neither Holmes 1985 nor McConnel 1991 explain the methods used to make medieval ring-type thimbles, i.e. cast, hammered, or soldered or unsoldered seamed sheet. However, Egan 1998 describes Nos 814-20 as 'soldered sheet rings', all of which are fragmented or/and distorted, and those that are illustrated do not show longitudinal seams, though the text with No. 819 (not catalogued here, but see Fig. 4) mentions 'solder traced' (Billingsgate Market 1983, site code BWB83, acc. 1135). MoL staff confirmed that Nos 816, 819 and 820, all found in an archaeologically stratified *c.*1350 - *c.*1400 context, actually do have longitudinal soldered seams – more accurately No. 819 has a longitudinal soldered scarfed seam. Using the London evidence, we can hypothesise that possibly the earliest ring-type thimbles used in Britain are those with longitudinal soldered or unsoldered seams. During this present study, many ring-type thimbles were examined, but only one with a longitudinal scarfed and lapped soldered seam is ascribed as *c.* early 13th – *c.* mid-15th century (No. 5). The aforesaid Amsterdam fragment is thought to probably have had a longitudinal soldered seam; its drilled pits are in columns thereby bolstering the hypothesis that this configuration is among the earliest (see above and below).

Circa mid-14th- – *c.* mid-15th-century ring-type thimbles with longitudinal seams that appear to have never been soldered are seemingly scarce in the British known record. Those herein (Nos 1-3) have pits in columns and lapped scarfed seams. This latter arrangement of seams raises a question; was it intentional? It certainly seems a plausible assumption, for the natural springiness of the metal facilitated easy adjustment to fit different size fingers. This hypothesis is strengthened by the chamfering angle of the seam edges being inconsistent with soldering them together. The aforesaid Chinese Warring States Period example is of this construction, which adds weight to the argument. Copper-alloy ring-type thimbles ascribed as *c.*1450 – *c.*1500 were without doubt produced in Nuremberg by both casting and longitudinal soldered seam sheet.

That other medieval copper-alloy ring-type thimbles were cast is certain and it is likely that hammering prevailed, too. Precisely how those hammered or cast were made into rings is unclear, but possibly after forming into domes, the crowns were sawn off.

Although English artisans may be responsible for some, these first ring-type thimbles found in Britain were possibly imported from mainland Europe, perhaps Nuremberg or elsewhere. Circa 15th-century very narrow ring-type thimbles are seemingly uncommon; with only one possible example noted during this present study (No. 17). The majority are quite tall and frequently were made with slightly or pronounced oblique bases or tops, features thought to provide a more comfortable fit on the finger (Nos 6-7, 10, 14, 16, 18, 21). A plausible alternative reason for oblique tops or bases is due to metal discs slipping during the hammering process (Greif 1986), and/or sloppy sawing. Oblique bases are noted on domed thimbles, too (see below). Other than drilling, punched pits also prevailed, either method in columns, frequently slightly oblique or irregular, random or a mixture of two configurations, while concentric circles or left-hand spirals appeared around the 15th century. As mentioned earlier, whatever the configuration, pits may totally cover the sides though circumferential upper and/or basal plain bands of varying depth is not uncommon. One or two circumferential basal engraved grooves and one around the upper rim are frequently evident, though they may be absent or run partially off the edge and therefore easily unnoticed. In Britain the earliest ring-types appear to be undecorated, though an example (No. 3) has geometric strapwork decoration. Decorated specimens from the 15th century seem to be uncommon though are known; one here (No. 22) features ornate patterns of circular pits. Of the hundred or so ring-type thimbles excavated in Corinth, several have simple patterns of drilled or punched circular pits (Fig. 3).

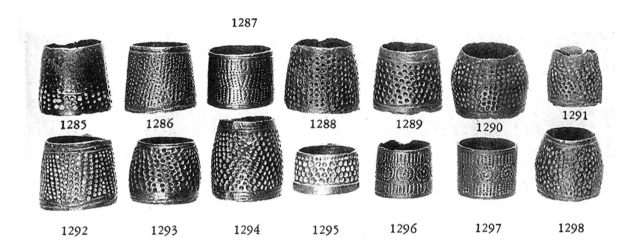

Figure 3. Ring-type copper-alloy thimbles *c.*9th – *c.*12th century, *Corinth*. (Note similarity with early ring-type thimbles found in Britain.) Top row: MF–7710, MF–7658, MF–7724, MF–8175, MF–7681, MF–5840, MF–6886 Bottom row: MF–4455, MF–7205, MF–6829, MF–4757, MF–2210, MF–5735, MF–5749. After Davidson 1952, Corinth 12, cat. 1285-1298, pl. 79. Photo copyright © and reproduced courtesy of the American School of Classical Studies at Athens, Corinth Excavation.

Figure 4. Soldered sheet copper-alloy ring-type thimble *c.*1350 – *c.*1400, *Billingsgate London*, 1983, Market site code BWB83, acc. 1135.
Note longitudinal sprung soldered scarfed seam.
Photo copyright © and reproduced courtesy of the MoL.

Figure 5. Ring-type copper-alloy thimbles *c.* early 13th century – *c.* 1450.

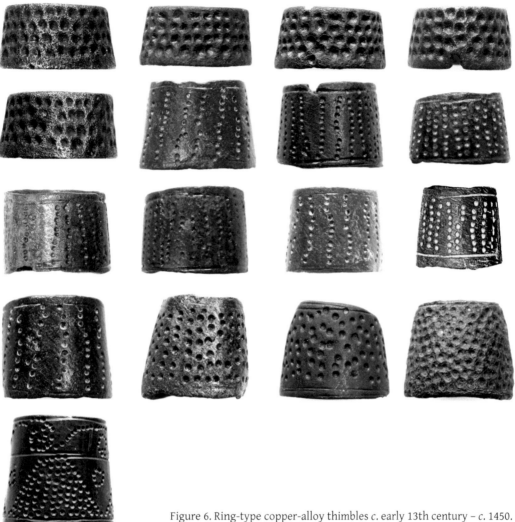

Figure 6. Ring-type copper-alloy thimbles *c.* early 13th century – *c.* 1450.

Ring-type thimbles with possibly unsoldered seams *c.* early 13th century – *c.*1450

Uncertain provenance. All are sheet copper-alloy with longitudinal possibly intentional unsoldered scarfed seams and drilled pits in columns, with circumferential plain bands and engraved grooves; unless specified otherwise, undecorated.

1. Ragged upper and basal edges, circumferential upper and basal plain bands each with one groove, D16mm H17.5mm. *Staffordshire.*

2. Circumferential upper and basal plain bands each with two grooves, D17.5mm H16.5mm. PAS BH-C71334. *Oxfordshire.*

3. Circumferential upper and basal plain bands each with one groove, three equidistant engraved bands of geometric oblique strapwork, D17.5mm H17mm. *North Dorset.*

Ring-type thimble with soldered seams *c.* early 13th century – *c.*1450

Uncertain provenance. Sheet copper-alloy with a longitudinal soldered butt seam, drilled pits in slightly oblique columns, with circumferential plain bands and engraved grooves and undecorated.

4. Sprung seam, circumferential upper and basal plain bands each with one groove, D25mm 16.5mm. *Wiltshire.*

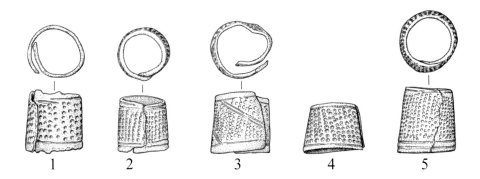

Ring-type thimble with soldered lapped and scarfed seam *c.* early 13th century – *c.*1450

Uncertain provenance. Sheet copper-alloy with longitudinal soldered lapped and scarfed seam, drilled pits in columns, with plain bands and circumferential engraved grooves and undecorated.

5. Seam edges are ragged, circumferential upper plain band has one groove and the basal, two; D15.5mm H17mm. *Buckinghamshire.*

Ring-type seamless thimbles, unless specified otherwise, all are *c.*15th century

Possibly from Nuremberg. All are copper-alloy; with or without circumferential plain bands and engraved grooves; unless specified otherwise, cast, with drilled pits, without makers' marks and undecorated.

6. Slightly oblique top, circumferential basal plain band, pits in columns, D18mm H15mm, *c.*13th – *c.*mid-14th century. *Dorset.*

7. Slightly oblique top; circumferential upper plain band with one groove, vestiges of circumferential basal plain band and one groove; pits in columns, D18.5mm H15.5mm, *c.*13th – *c.*mid-14th century. *South Wiltshire.*

8. Straight sides, circumferential upper and basal narrow plain bands each with one groove, pits in columns, D18.5mm H13mm, *c.*13th – *c.*mid-14th century. *South Somerset.*

9. Circumferential upper and basal plain bands each with one groove, pits in irregular columns, D20mm H15mm, *c.*13th – *c.*mid-14th century. *South Somerset.*

10. Oblique top; circumferential basal plain band with one complete groove and vestiges of a second, vestiges of an upper plain band and one groove, random pits, D21mm H18.5mm, *c.*13th – *c.*mid-14th. *South Somerset.*

11. Five concentric circles of pits, D17mm H10mm. *South Lincolnshire.*

12. Four concentric circles of pits, D15mm H8mm. *South Lincolnshire.*

13. Circumferential basal plain band, four concentric circles of pits; D19.5mm H10mm. *South Somerset.*

14. Slightly oblique top; circumferential basal plain band, four concentric circles of pits; D17mm H10mm. *South Somerset.*

15. Circumferential basal plain band, four concentric circles of pits; D19.5mm H10.5mm. *South Lincolnshire.*

16. Slightly oblique top, circumferential upper and basal plain bands, four concentric circles of pits, D21.4mm H11.5mm. *South Lincolnshire.*

17. Probably hammered, height varies, slightly concave sides; internal and external curvilinear grooves, the inner easily mistaken for a soldered scarfed seam; a left-hand spiral of crude probable punched circular pits, some of which resemble annulets; some pits probably are worn away, H0.6mm D19mm. PAS CORN-152011. *Cornwall.*

18. Slightly oblique top, vestige of circumferential upper plain band and basal plain band with one deep groove, seven concentric circles of pits, D19mm H15.5mm. *Buckinghamshire.*

19. Circumferential upper narrow plain band and basal plain band with one deep groove, left-hand spiral of pits, D19mm H15.5mm. *South Somerset.*

20. Circumferential basal plain band with two grooves, the upper one faint; left-hand spiral of pits; D21mm H14.5mm. *South Wiltshire.*

21. Oblique top; one circumferential upper and one basal groove; left-hand spiral of pits, D21mm H18.2mm. *Oxfordshire.*

22. Fairly straight sides divided by three circumferential grooves, upper, basal and another two-thirds up from the base; pits form running S-scrolls in the upper section of the sides and repeating triangles with annulets between, in the lower; D20.5mm H19mm. *South East Dorset.*

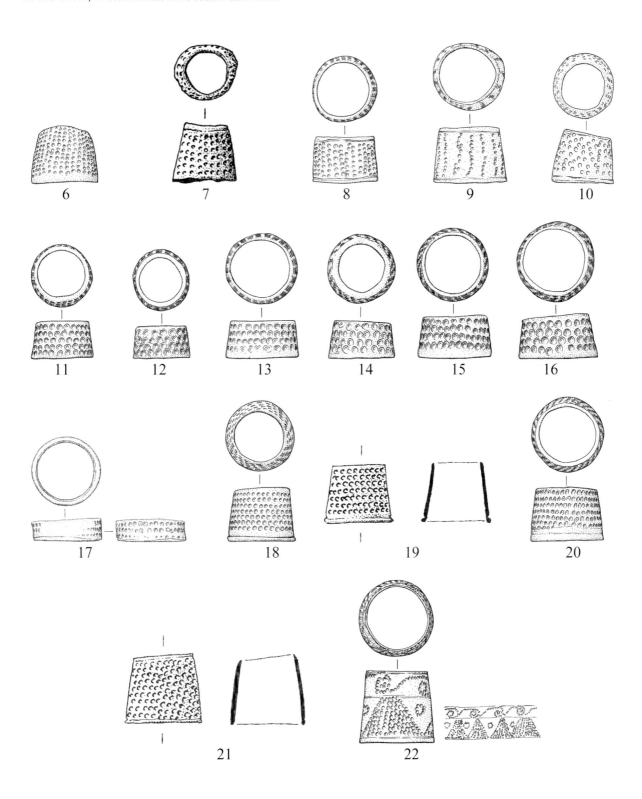

Ring-type seamless thimbles *c.* 1450 – *c.* 1600

Apart from Nuremberg, copper-alloy ring-type thimbles ascribed as *c.*1450 – *c.*1600 also were probably produced in the Netherlands and England by casting or hammering sheet metal. Cast ring-type thimbles may feature thicker sides than those hammered from sheet, though differentiating the two manufactory techniques can be difficult. Oblique tops or bases appear uncommon and are less acute. Pits are circular, primarily drilled but sometimes punched, and configured in concentric circles or from about 1550, right-hand spirals. Similarly, pits may completely cover the sides though some have circumferential upper and/or basal plain bands of varying depth.

Reliable archaeological evidence from Amsterdam explains that around the middle of the 16th century, other than circular and oval, shapes of pits became more varied, i.e. rectangular/square, triangular, D-shape, reversed D-shape or a combination of two shapes, configured primarily in right-hand spirals, and to a lesser extent, concentric circles or columns. Many of these ring-types are crude and narrow, with two to four bands of pits, while, conversely, others are quite tall. A circumferential basal and/or upper plain band with one or two engraved grooves is noted on many though plain bands without grooves is not unusual. White-metal (probably tin) or a black coating is apparent on some though other decoration is uncommon, however, basal and upper bands, or just basal, of simple engraving or punchwork, is known (Nos 32-33). Not all of the Amsterdam archaeologically excavated ring-type thimbles were necessarily Dutch-made, without doubt some are from Nuremberg or elsewhere. This creates a problem with identification because certain ring-types produced in any of these places are similar. Nuremberg-made ring-type thimbles found in that city and now in Museum I22I20I18I Kühnertsgasse, Nuremberg confirms the only difference is many bear a maker's mark (Nos 34-48, 55) (see below).

Mid-16th-century ring-types with confirmed longitudinal soldered seams appear to be virtually unrecorded by archaeology; perhaps they are but ascribed as medieval; none are seemingly recorded as found archaeologically in London (Egan 2005). This apparent paucity from archaeological sites of early post-medieval soldered-seam sheet ring-type thimbles also extends into detecting finds, and this present study revealed only six (Nos 49-55). Longitudinal soldered seams may be butt or scarfed. A repair to a split side is apparent on the inside of No. 55.

By 1494 Nuremberg thimble-makers were incorporated into the Guild of Coppersmiths and thereafter had to cast their own domed thimbles (see below). Whether this included ring-types is unclear, but is probable. No doubt silver ring-type thimbles were made too, though proven 15th-century examples appear absent from the known record.

The Nuremberg Guild required all masters (makers) to acquire a tool (punch) for marking their wares and *c.*1520 makers' marks began to be punched on thimbles – both ring-type and domed – made in Nuremberg. Frustratingly, however, not every maker complied. On ring-types with right-hand spiralled pits, such marks are usually placed at the base where the spiral starts, though sometimes further around or even on a basal groove or ridge (Nos 34-48, 55). Greif 1986 states that from the 16th century until the 18th, after passing the masters' exam, each Nuremberg thimble-maker was required to punch his mark on a metal sheet (in England known as a 'touch plate'). After the Nuremberg Guild was dissolved in the 18th century the touch plate vanished. Whether Greif 1986 meant makers' marks were applied to both the touch plate and thimbles for the whole of the 17th century and all or part of the 18th is unclear. Holmes 1988, however, contradicts Greif by stating that from *c.*1520 to *c.*1620 many Nuremberg copper-alloy ring-type and domed thimbles were punched with a maker's mark. Of the two, who is correct is uncertain therefore stamping of marks may have extended into the 18th century. Ring-type thimbles with makers' marks and confidently ascribed as post 1650, appear absent from the known record. Ten ring-type thimbles, several punched with a maker's mark, and three domed (all presumably Nuremberg products, see below) were recovered from the *Mary Rose* sunk off Portsmouth in 1545 (see below).

Figure 7. Ring-type copper-alloy and silver thimbles
c.1450 – c.1600.

Despite us knowing that the Nuremberg Thimble-makers' Guild required all thimbles made in that city to be punched with the respective maker's mark, with the exception of several, we have no idea which mark belonged to which thimble-maker (see below). A caveat is therefore prudent – should some makers' marks assumed as Nuremberg's really be credited to thimble-makers elsewhere in Europe (see below)? As there is no record of any other regulatory guilds for thimble-making in Europe at this time, here such marks are tentatively credited to Nuremberg. This difficulty with identifying makers' marks is compounded by a requirement for journeymen (those who have completed an apprenticeship but not yet passed the masters' exam) and contractors, e.g. wholesalers who dealt with pieceworkers, also punching their respective marks on thimbles worked on by them. Supposed Nuremberg ring-type thimbles punched with marks of two separate craftsmen are uncommon, therefore whether this practice was generally complied with seems doubtful.

Ring-type seamless thimbles *c.*1520 – *c.*1600

Possibly from Nuremberg. All are copper-alloy, probably cast, with punched pits; with or without circumferential plain bands and engraved grooves, without makers' marks and unless specified otherwise, undecorated.

23. Circumferential upper and basal plain bands, four concentric circles of square pits; D19.5mm H11mm. *South West Wiltshire.*

24. Circumferential upper and basal plain bands each with one groove, two concentric circles of triangular pits, D17mm H10mm. PAS CORN-99B300. *Cornwall.*

25. Small dent in upper rim, circumferential upper and basal plain bands each with one groove, the basal wide and deep; three concentric circles of triangular pits, D19mm H11mm. PAS IOW-605010. *Isle of Wight.*

26. Circumferential upper and basal plain bands each with one groove, right-hand spiral of square pits, D17mm H11mm. *South East Lincolnshire.*

27. Circumferential basal plain band with one groove, right-hand spiral of square pits, D17 H11mm. *South East Lincolnshire.*

28. Circumferential basal plain band with one groove, right-hand spiral of reversed D-shaped/triangular pits, D19.5mm H11mm. *South West Wiltshire.*

29. Circumferential upper and basal plain bands each with one groove, right-hand spiral of triangular pits, D21mm H12mm. *South Lincolnshire.*

30. Possibly a domed thimble with the crown removed; circumferential basal plain band with one groove, right-hand spiral of elongated oval pits; an upper lateral inwards upper rim with identical pits; D15mm H13.5mm. *South West Wiltshire.*

31. Circumferential upper and basal plain bands, the upper punched with repeating oval pits and the basal similar repeating slightly larger oval pits between two grooves, right-hand spiral of oval pits, D20.66mm H17.42mm. PAS IOW-1C5226. *Isle of Wight.*

32. Possibly hammered, distorted upper rim; circumferential upper and basal plain bands, the upper with vestiges of repeating punched dots, and the basal punched repeating addorsed crescents between two grooves, right-hand spiral of square pits, D17.5mm H17.8mm. *South Somerset.*

33. Possibly hammered; circumferential upper and basal bands, the upper with one groove and repeating punched voided ovals, and the basal, punched repeating addorsed voided crescents between two engraved grooves; right-hand spiral of triangular pits; D18mm H16mm. PAS LIN-0C06B6. *Lincolnshire.*

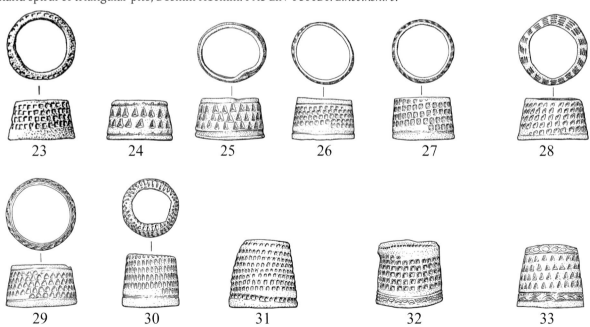

Ring-type seamless thimbles *c*.1520 - *c*.1600

Probably from Nuremberg. All are copper-alloy; with makers' marks; unless specified otherwise, cast; with punched pits, with or without circumferential plain bands and engraved grooves and undecorated.

34. Ragged upper and basal edges, circumferential upper and basal plain bands, right-hand spiral of square pits (recorded as triangular by PAS but interpreted as square by illustrator), maker's mark away from start of spiral – S flanked each side with an I in a square cartouche, D21mm H12mm. PAS HAMP-695395. *East Dorset.*

35. Circumferential basal plain band, right-hand spiral of circular pits, indeterminate maker's mark at start of spiral, D16.5mm H9.5mm. *South Lincolnshire.*

36. Circumferential basal plain band, right-hand spiral of circular pits, indeterminate maker's mark at start of spiral, D19.2mm H10.5mm. *South Lincolnshire.*

37. Right-hand spiral of square pits; maker's mark at start of spiral – Latin cross in an asymmetrical cartouche, D20mm H11mm. PAS SF-B82E37. *Suffolk.*

38. Circumferential basal plain band, right-hand spiral of square pits; maker's mark away from start of spiral – Latin cross in an asymmetrical cartouche, D20.3mm H11.5mm. *South Somerset.*

39. PAS report states cast though two longitudinal creases suggest perhaps hammered, though a top to bottom split could be a sprung soldered seam; circumferential upper and basal plain bands, right-hand spiral of circular pits; maker's mark at start of spiral resembles a hockey stick, possibly a partially erased S, D18mm H20mm. PAS LON-16A7A2. *London.*

40. Circumferential basal plain band with one groove, right-hand spiral of triangular pits; indeterminate maker's mark in a pentagonal cartouche at start of spiral – possibly as Nos 36, 41, D21mm H12mm. UKDFD 9921. *Kent.*

41. Circumferential basal plain band with one deep groove, right-hand spiral of rectangular pits; maker's mark at start of spiral – possibly a crown in a pentagonal cartouche, D20mm H10.5mm. *Buckinghamshire.*

42. Circumferential basal plain band with one engraved deep groove, right-hand spiral of square pits; maker's mark at start of spiral – Latin cross in an asymmetrical cartouche, D19mm H10mm. *South Lincolnshire.*

43. Possibly hammered, upper rim slightly damaged, circumferential upper and basal bands each with a repeating band of punched circular pits, right-hand spiral of circular pits; maker's mark at start of spiral – five-pointed star in a circular cartouche, D21mm H15mm. UKDFD 16576. *Somerset.*

44. Possibly hammered; circumferential upper and basal plain bands, each with one deep groove and bordered by shallow ridges, the upper has repeating punched oval-and-dot motifs and the basal indistinct punched repeating crescents; right-hand spiral of triangular pits; maker's mark at start of spiral – (?) fish (?) flask in an incomplete asymmetrical cartouche, D19.5mm H17mm. *Buckinghamshire.*

45. Possibly hammered, circumferential upper and basal plain bands, each with one deep groove, the upper with repeating punched crescents and pellets; the basal band, which is flanked each side with a ridge, is segmented by punched vertical lines and addorsed voided crescents; right-hand spiral of circular pits, maker's mark at start of spiral – B B each letter in a crescentic cartouche, D21.5mm H17mm. PAS DOR-BF4691. *Dorset.*

46. Possibly hammered, circumferential upper and basal plain bands, both with one deep groove flanked each side with a ridge, the basal groove has repeating punched alternate annulets and bars; right-hand spiral of circular pits; maker's mark at start of spiral – sprig, D19mm H15mm. *South Lincolnshire.*

47. Possibly hammered, circumferential upper and basal plain bands, the upper with one deep groove flanked each side with a ridge; the basal band has two grooves, the lowest wide and deep and flanked each side with a ridge; a right-hand spiral of circular pits; maker's mark at start of spiral – crescent; D28mm H23.4mm. *Somerset.*

48. Circumferential upper and basal plain bands, the upper with one groove, the basal is wider with one deep groove flanked each side with a ridge; right-hand spiral of rectangular pits; maker's mark on the basal upper ridge – S S configured horizontally head-to-tail, D20mm H19mm. UKDFD 36157. *Essex.*

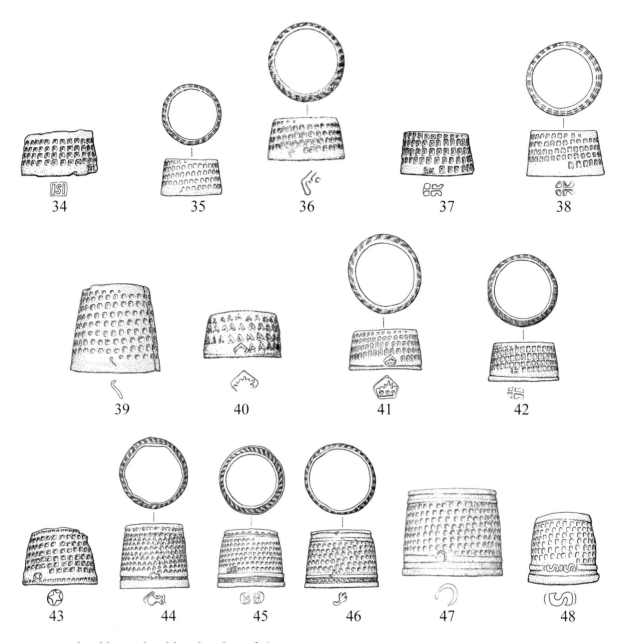

Ring-type thimbles with soldered and scarfed seams *c.*1520 – *c.*1600

Probably from Nuremberg. All are sheet copper-alloy with longitudinal soldered scarfed seams; with punched pits, with or without circumferential plain bands and engraved grooves, undecorated; unless specified otherwise, without makers' marks.

49. Scarfed seam, right-hand spiral of triangular pits, D22mm H12mm. UKDFD 47639. *Lincolnshire*

50. Sprung scarfed seam; circumferential upper and basal plain bands, the upper with a vestige of one groove, and basal one groove; right-hand spiral of square pits, D20mm H11mm. UKDFD-39558. *Essex.*

51. Butt seam, circumferential upper and basal plain bands, the basal with two grooves; five concentric circles of drilled pits; D10.5mm H14mm. *South Devon.*

52. Butt seam; circumferential upper and basal plain bands, the upper with two grooves, the basal one deep, making a distinct rim; six concentric circles of drilled pits; D17mm H14.5mm. *South Somerset.*

53. Sprung scarfed seam retaining solder residue; circumferential upper and basal plain bands, each with one groove, the basal one deep, making a distinct rim; six concentric circles of drilled pits; D19mm H14mm. PAS SF6273. *Suffolk.*

54. Possibly composite two-piece with a butt seam; a possible separately soldered pronounced basal rim (if so, an unusual feature on thimbles of this period) with white-metal coating and a small pit on the outside edge; left-hand spiral of probably circular pits; D25mm H19.5mm. PAS IOW-0B2034. *Isle of Wight.*

Ring-type thimble with soldered, scarfed and lapped seams *c.*1520 – *c.*1600

Probably from Nuremberg. Sheet copper-alloy with longitudinal soldered scarfed and lapped seams, with circumferential plain bands and engraved grooves, with maker's mark, and undecorated.

55. Evidence of a repair inside, circumferential upper and basal plain bands, each with two grooves flanked both sides by ridges; right-hand spiral of square pits; maker's mark across the groove near the start of spiral – R; D20mm H15.5mm. *South Somerset.*

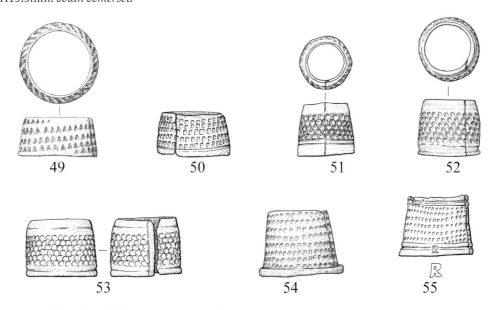

Ring-type seamless thimbles *c.*1600 – *c.*19th century

Did early to late 17th-century English artisans produce silver or copper-alloy sheet ring-type thimbles in similar designs as their domed counterparts (see below)? Holmes 1985 pp 55 mentions one found in the USA, which he describes as 'topless' while the caption reads 'sewing ring'. These statements are frustratingly ambiguous – is it a composite domed thimble that has lost its crown or a true ring-type thimble? No mention is made whether it is hammered or has a longitudinal soldered seam. The present writer has studied many composite sheet silver and sheet copper-alloy domed thimbles from this period; excavated examples frequently lack a crown but they all feature a longitudinal soldered seam which may be butt, scarfed or scarfed and lapped. Magnification of horizontal rims will reveal whether they are angled at almost 45° to the sides, i.e. bevelled inwards; a bevelled rim is always evidence of a lost crown. Conversely, crownless thimbles with completely smooth 90° butt rims may mean they are actually ring-types. Any rim retaining solder residue or is rough may suggest a lost crown. Caution is therefore advised when determining whether thimbles of this type are really ring-types or incomplete composite domed – this ambiguity means that herein some classed as domed actually may be ring-types. An unusual composite three-piece sheet silver ring-type thimble here (No. 67) is possibly late 16th century or early 17th though its place of manufacture is unknown.

Both the Dutch and English produced ring-type thimbles by casting during the 17th and 18th centuries and for many it is virtually impossible to differentiate between them; notwithstanding the majority found in Britain are likely to be Dutch. These ring-types may lack circumferential upper or basal plain bands, or have only one, usually the upper (No 56). Typically, such plain bands feature circumferential engraved grooves, often both upper and basal, though sometimes are absent. Frequently these grooves are deep – the lowest and uppermost creating rims. Basal rims, with or without grooves, may be very pronounced or lesser so (Nos 56-59, 61-64). As mentioned above, it is this style of ring-type that is similar to some made in Nuremberg. These characteristic features are also mirrored on Dutch Holmes' Type I composite and Dutch or English (John Lofting) Holmes' Type II cast domed thimbles too (see below). Ring-type thimbles with mechanically knurled pits are also recorded but are less common (No. 66). Interestingly, the *Register of 16th- – 18th-century Patents for Inventions* in the Netherlands National Archive has no record of who invented the device for impressing knurled pits on thimbles. However, Gerart van Slangenborch, a Dutch thimble-maker resident in Amsterdam, in 1608 sold his invention of a multiple knurling wheel for thimbles (Langedijk and Boon 1999). The earliest knurling device impressed circular pits, but by the late 17th century lozenge-shaped pits were used as well. Mechanical knurling is uniform and usually but not always easily differentiated from hand-punched pits. Whether the Dutch produced Holmes' Type I sheet ring-type thimbles with longitudinal soldered seams is uncertain.

Copper-alloy ring-type thimbles, and domed too, were recovered by marine archaeologists from the wreck of the Dutch East Indiaman *De Liefde* (*The Love*) which in 1711, while bound for the Orient via the Cape of Good Hope, foundered on the Out Skerries, Shetland Isles. Whether these thimbles were cargo, crew effects or ship's equipment is unclear. Whatever, a selection is now in the Shetland Museum and Archive (Figs 8, 30). The domed examples are Dutch Holmes' Type II *c*.1650 – *c*.1730 (see below) while the ring-types are as Nos 56-59 herein.

Pits on all forms are punched circular and configured in right-hand spirals, concentric circles or, uncommonly, columns, which differ from mechanically knurled pits usually seen on Dutch and English Holmes' Types I and II (see below). In 1712 Bernhard von der Becke established a thimble mill at Sundwig, North Rhine-Westphalia, Germany, where ring-types, presumably of copper alloy, were produced. Precisely how they were made is unrecorded (Holmes 1988), and what they look like is uncertain.

John Lofting possibly produced cast one-piece ring-type thimbles and Holmes 1985 provides evidence that Lofting manufactured sheet ring-types with longitudinal soldered butt-seams though this is unproven. If Lofting, or someone else, did, presumably they were similarly knurled as Holmes' Type III domed thimbles (see below). Herein No. 256 is a contender for a possible mechanically knurled sheet ring-type thimble with a sprung longitudinal soldered butt seam though it could be a knurled sheet composite two-piece domed thimble that has lost its crown (see below).

Figure 8. Dutch cast copper-alloy ring-type thimble from the Dutch East Indiaman *De Liefde* 18th century. Note mechanically knurled circular pits, upper circumferential groove and pronounced basal rim. Photo copyright © Lewis Murray and reproduced courtesy of Shetland Museum and Archive.

We know that from *c*.1520 until *c*.1620 many ring-type thimbles made in Nuremberg carried a punched maker's mark. Confusingly, from the first half of the 17th century some Dutch-made thimbles of both kinds were marked, too, but there is no record of to whom such marks are attributed (Langedijk and Boon 1999). Names of known Dutch thimble-makers and dates when operating and/or mentioned are: Gerart van Slangenborch 1608; Baptista van Regemorter *c*.1608–13; Jacob Seyne 1613; Claes Schot 1620; Jacob Schot 1622-41 (son of Claes Schot); Marichgen Petersdr 1628 (wife of Claes Schot) and her other four sons; the Van Rijssel family *c*.1650 until the end of the 18th century; Willem van Rijssel 1686-1736; Aelbert van Rijssel 1686–1736 (father of Willem van Rijssel); Hendrik Schot 1686-1736; Beernt van Beeckum 1686-1736; Jan Carel Matthes 1750–82 (Langedijk and Boon 1999).

Figure 9. Ring-type copper-alloy and white-metal coated malleable iron/steel thimbles c.17th – c.18th century.

About 1812 the Joh. Caspar Rumpe Works at Altena, also North Rhine-Westphalia, is known to have been producing composite two-piece ring-type thimbles made from rolled malleable iron sheeting lined inside with rolled copper-alloy sheeting, each section with a longitudinal soldered butt-seam. These ring-types may feature a circumferential basal rim. Pits are either punched (various shapes) or drilled and configured in concentric circles. Circumferential basal and upper engraved lines are usual and white-metal coating (probably tin) was used to inhibit corrosion. This present study revealed no composite malleable iron/steel and copper-alloy ring-type thimbles, presumably due to their poor survival in the soil. A white-metal coated (probably tin) iron specimen here (No. 65) features a longitudinal soldered scarfed butt seam, and is tentatively ascribed as c.17th – c.18th century.

Ring-type seamless thimbles c.17th – c.18th century

Probably from the Netherlands. All are cast copper-alloy with drilled pits, with or without circumferential engraved grooves; unless specified otherwise, undecorated.

56. Small nick in upper rim, circumferential upper plain band, seven concentric circles of pits, pronounced basal rim, D22mm H15mm. *South Somerset.*

57. Circumferential upper recessed plain band with one groove, seven concentric circles of pits, pronounced basal rim, D18mm H14mm. UKDFD-37461. *Suffolk.*

58. Circumferential upper and basal plain bands, the upper with one groove; seven concentric circles of pits; pronounced basal rim, D20mm H15mm. *South Somerset.*

59. Circumferential upper and basal plain bands, the upper with two deep grooves and a central ridge, and the basal, one groove; six concentric circles of pits, pronounced basal rim, D19mm H16mm. *South Somerset.*

60. Slightly convex sides, circumferential upper and basal plain bands, the upper has one groove punched with repeating tiny ring-and-dot motifs, and the basal two grooves with a median ridge; four irregular concentric circles of pits, D17mm H14mm. PAS SUSS-12E615. *East Sussex.*

61. Circumferential upper and basal plain bands, each with one deep groove flanked each side with a ridge, seven concentric circles of pits, D19mm H17mm. *South Somerset.*

62. Circumferential upper and basal plain bands, the upper with one groove and the basal two flanked each side with a ridge; seven concentric circles of large pits, D17mm H17mm. UKDFD 10471. *Dorset.*

63. Convex sides; circumferential upper and basal plain bands, the upper with one groove and basal two with a median ridge, five concentric circles of pits; a pronounced basal rim, D19mm H14mm. UKDFD 30901. *Gloucestershire.*

64. Convex sides, circumferential upper and basal plain bands, the upper with three grooves and a pronounced rim and the basal one groove; six concentric circles of pits; a pronounced basal rim, D13.5mm H13.5mm. UKDFD-10254. *Lancashire.*

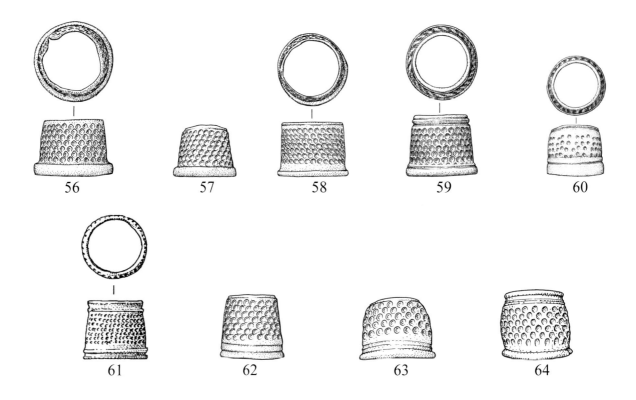

56   57   58   59   60

61   62   63   64

Ring-type thimbles with soldered seams *c.* 17th – *c.*18th century

Probably from the Netherlands or England. With circumferential plain bands and engraved grooves; unless specified otherwise, all are sheet copper-alloy with longitudinal soldered butt seams; and undecorated.

65. Heavy-gauge malleable iron, several cracks around the upper rim, scarfed seam, white-metal coated (? tin); circumferential upper and basal plain bands, the upper with two faint grooves, and basal two deeper grooves with a median ridge; five irregular concentric circles of probable drilled pits; a slightly pronounced basal rim with engraved repeating transverse grooves; D20mm H14.5mm. *South Somerset.*

66. Scarfed seam; circumferential upper and basal plain bands, the upper with one groove, and basal three, one faint; mechanically knurled circular pits; D17.4mm H20.5mm. *Buckinghamshire.*

67. Sheet silver, composite three-piece with longitudinal and horizontal indeterminate seams; the circumferential separate soldered upper rim resembles a plain band with two grooves and crenulations, a circumferential separate soldered basal plain band has two grooves, columns of probable punched circular pits; D18mm H19.mm. *(?) Norfolk.*

65   66   67

Metal Domed Thimbles

Domed thimbles *c*.12th century – *c*.1400

The aforesaid Hispano-Moresque medieval large cast copper-alloy domed thimble is possibly the earliest domed thimble excavated from British soil by a detectorist (No. 68 and Fig. 11). Holmes 1985 states Museo Arqueologico, Madrid has two such thimbles that may date from as early as the 10th century AD; each of which is inscribed 'Made by Al-Sayib'. Moorish General Tariq ibn Ziyad, in AD 711, under orders of Umayyad Caliph Al-Walid, successfully conquered the Iberian Peninsular (modern Spain), and the Moors ruled there for 800 years. If these domed thimbles were manufactured in the aforesaid Cordoba from the 10th century, feasibly they continued to be produced there until the end of the Moorish rule in the 15th century. Holmes 1985 quotes a 12th-century date for his thimble; therefore the same attribution is possible for the example found in Britain. Although not uncommon finds in Spain and North Africa, in this country No. 68 is the only detector-found example in the known record. Its incomplete and corroded condition is not a trustworthy indicator of age or its length of disposition in the ground.

Another seemingly unusual recovery in Britain, and the known record's only detectorist-found example, is a Turko-Slavic (eastern Mediterranean and eastern Europe) substantial cast copper-alloy domed thimble possibly ascribed as early as the 13th century but perhaps as late as the 17th (No. 69 and Fig. 11).

Aside the aforesaid Moorish domed thimble, the earliest copper-alloy domed thimbles regularly found in Britain possibly date from *c*.1330 – *c*.1400 and are distinctive by being well-cast, extremely small, shallow and lightweight; how they stayed on the finger is difficult to comprehend. Two basic shapes are apparent, each comparable with one of the two styles of skep, the late Iron Age wicker-and-daub beehive and later medieval straw version, hence why they are frequently called 'skeps' or 'beehives' (Nos 70-86). The word skep derives from the Old English *sceppe*, 'basket, from the Old Norse *skeppa*, 'basket, bushel'. One type has sides that fairly quickly slope inwards towards the crown while the sides and crown of the other are more rounded, resembling an acorn cup, thereby providing the name 'acorn-cup'. Crowns, which sometimes feature a teat-like apex (Nos 70, 77-78), may be covered with pits while others are tonsured. Pits are circular and necessarily minute and appear drilled on the smaller specimens and drilled or punched on larger versions. Several configurations of pits are noted, namely: columns on the sides up to an engraved circumferential groove, columns on the sides that extend over the crown up to a tonsure; columns, frequently slightly oblique or irregular, on the sides and concentric circles on the crowns up to a tonsure; sides with columns, frequently slightly oblique or irregular, on the lower section and concentric circles on the upper, and concentric circles on the crown up to a tonsure; concentric circles on the sides and the crown up to a tonsure; or a left-hand spiral on the sides and concentric circles on the crown up to a tonsure. Circumferential basal plain bands with either one or two engraved grooves feature on many.

Proof that skeps were made in England is absent and they are perhaps products of Nuremberg though this is conjecture; makers' marks are absent. The known record has examples of small skeps with creased sides, indicating the hammering method prevailed too – confirmed by Egan 1998 no 821, securely dated as *c*.1330 – *c*.1380. Although none with such a feature were noted during this present study, some here may have been hammered, but apart from those with a small hole in the crown (Nos 70, 73-79, 81-82, 85), implying they were perhaps cast; differentiating the two techniques is difficult.

Decorated skeps are seemingly scarce though one herein (No. 82) is engraved with a circle on its crown, and geometric strapwork, with or without engraved borders, is noted on several (Nos 83-86). Strapwork may be have been adopted by Nuremberg thimble-makers as their interpretation of the decoration found on Hama, Syrian, (Abbasid-Levantine) domed thimbles possibly brought home by returning Crusaders.

Figure 10. Domed copper-alloy (aka acorn cup) thimbles *c*.1330 – *c*.1400.

Cast copper-alloy carinated or faceted domed thimbles, some with geometric strapwork, either with or without engraved linear borders, possibly from Nuremberg's early period, c.1330 – c.1400 (Nos 87-91), are increasingly evident in the known record in Britain. They are conveniently comparable with skeps though their footprint is either hexagonal, septfoil, octagonal, polygonal or circular; but the sides are still carinated. A seemingly unusual slightly taller example is polygonal and narrower in diameter than the others here (No. 87). Likewise, they may have similar features as the preceding skeps.

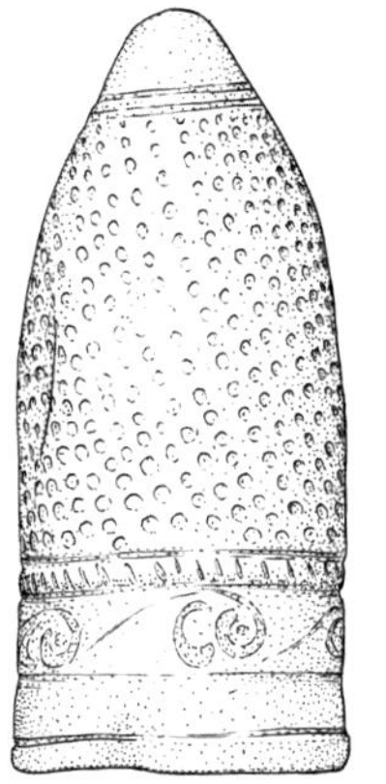

Domed thimble c.12th century – c.1400

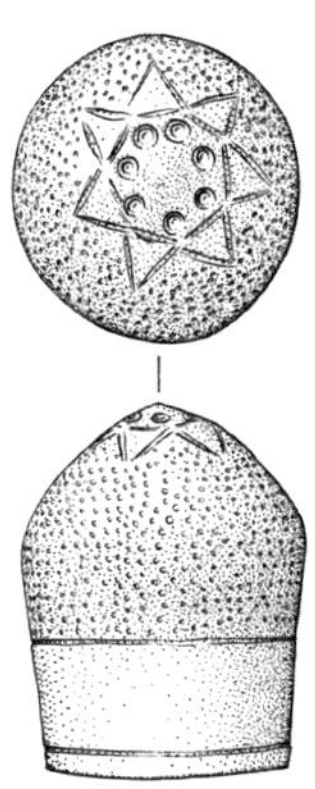

From Cordoba, Spain. Hispano-Moresque. Cast copper-alloy with drilled pits, circumferential plain bands and engraved grooves and decorated.

68. Section of side broken off and distorted; circumferential basal wide band has four grooves creating two plain bands, one with running spirals, and one hatched; a tonsured crown with two basal grooves; pits in concentric circles on the sides, D24.5mm H52.5mm. *Hampshire.*

Domed thimble c.13th – c.17th century

From the Eastern Mediterranean or Eastern Europe. Turko-Slavic. Cast copper-alloy with probably punched pits, circumferential plain bands and engraved grooves and decorated.

69. Bulbous, a circumferential basal plain band with two grooves; a continuous left-hand spiral of circular pits on the sides and crown, crown engraved with a seven-pointed star around a circle and seven drilled large pits; D20mm H26mm. *Kent.*

68   69

Figure 11. Hispano-Moresque and Turko-Slavic domed thimbles

Domed skep (aka acorn cup) thimbles c.1330 – c.1400

All possibly from Nuremberg. All are cast copper-alloy, with or without circumferential plain bands and engraved grooves; unless specified otherwise, with drilled pits and undecorated. Geometric strapwork decoration on four is either with or without engraved outlines.

70. A circumferential basal plain band, pits in oblique columns on the sides and three concentric circles on a tonsured pierced teat crown, D17mm H14mm. *South West Wiltshire.*

71. A circumferential basal plain band with one groove, pits in columns extending two thirds of the way up the sides and eight concentric circles on a tonsured crown, D17mm H16mm. *South West Wiltshire.*

72. A circumferential basal plain band with two grooves, pits in columns on the sides and four concentric circles on a tonsured crown, D14.5mm H14.6mm. *South West Dorset.*

73. A circumferential basal plain band with two grooves, pits in columns on the sides and three concentric circles on a tonsured pierced crown, D14.5mm H14.6mm. *South West Dorset.*

74. A circumferential basal narrow plain band with one groove, pits in columns on the sides and five concentric circles on a tonsured pierced crown, D13.5mm H11.4mm. *South West Wiltshire.*

75. A circumferential basal plain band with one groove, pits in columns on the sides and three concentric circles on a tonsured pierced crown, D14mm H11mm. *South West Lincolnshire.*

76. A circumferential basal plain band with two grooves, pits in columns on the sides and five concentric circles on a tonsured pierced crown, D17mm H13.3mm. *Buckinghamshire.*

77. A circumferential basal plain band with one groove, pits in columns on the sides and five concentric circles on a tonsured pierced teat crown, D17mm H12mm. UKDFD 520. *Worcestershire.*

78. A circumferential basal plain band with one groove, pits in columns on the sides and three concentric circles on a tonsured pierced teat crown, D16mm H14mm. *Buckinghamshire.*

79. A circumferential basal plain band with one groove, pits in columns on the sides and three concentric circles on a tonsured pierced crown, D17.5mm H13.5mm. *South West Wiltshire.*

80. Possibly hammered, creases in the sides, a circumferential basal plain band with two grooves, pits in irregular columns on the sides and five irregular concentric circles on the crown; D17.8mm H16.5mm. *South West Wiltshire.*

81. A circumferential basal plain band with one groove, pits in columns on the sides, a tonsured pierced crown with a groove separating the side pits from the tonsure, D15.6mm H10.7mm. PAS BH-49EA23. *Oxfordshire.*

82. A circumferential basal plain band with one groove, pits in columns on the sides and four concentric circles on a tonsured pierced crown with an engraved split circle around the hole, D17.2mm H15mm. PAS BERK-998980. *Hertfordshire.*

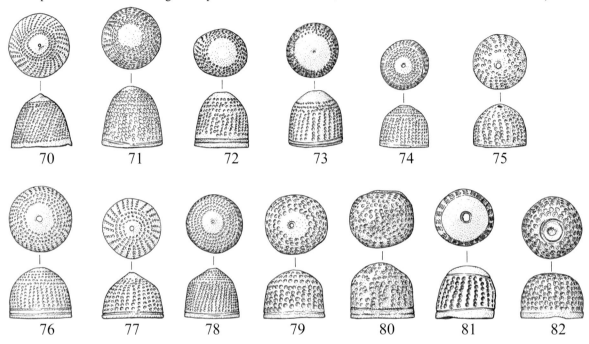

83. A circumferential basal plain band with one deep groove creating a rim, pits in oblique columns on the sides and four concentric circles on a tonsured crown, geometric zigzag strapwork is without outlines, D17.5mm H13.5mm. *South Gloucestershire.*

84. Sides split, distorted and abraded; a circumferential basal plain band, pits in columns on the sides up to a tonsured crown marked with seven irregularly spaced circular pits perhaps caused by a needle, outlined geometric strapwork, D17mm H14mm. *West Buckinghamshire.*

85. A circumferential basal plain band with one groove, a second groove separates the sides from the pierced crown; pits in columns on the sides and rows on the crown, outlined geometric strapwork divides the sides into rectangles and triangles on the crown, the crown strapwork resembles a saltire; D15mm H11mm. *South West Wiltshire.*

86. Pits in columns on the sides and four concentric circles on a tonsured crown; outlined geometric strapwork comparable with No. 85 though the crown has five radiating arms, D16.2mm H7.8mm. *South West Wiltshire.*

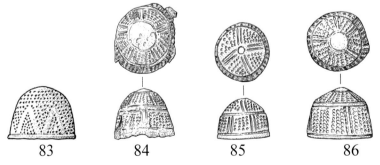

Domed skep (aka acorn cup) carinated / faceted thimbles *c.*1330 – *c.*1400

All possibly from Nuremberg. All are cast copper-alloy with carinated or faceted sides and crowns; drilled pits; with or without circumferential plain bands and engraved grooves, unless specified otherwise, undecorated. Geometric strapwork decoration on four is either with or without engraved outlines.

87. Polygonal footprint, a circumferential basal plain band with one groove, pits in columns on the sides and four concentric circles on a tonsured pierced teat crown; D14mm H15mm. *South Lincolnshire.*

88. Septfoil footprint, carinated sides and tonsured crown, a circumferential basal plain band with two grooves; pits in columns, geometric strapwork is without outlines and forms pentagonal panels on the sides, the crown strapwork resembles a centrally pierced seven-spoked wheel; D16.5mm H14mm. *South Lincolnshire.*

89. Circular footprint, carinated sides and crown, a vestige of a basal groove; pits in columns, outlined geometric strapwork forms domed panels on the sides and subtriangular on a tonsured crown; the crown strapwork resembles a centrally pierced eight-spoked wheel; D15.3mm H12.2mm. *Dorset.*

90. Split in side and distorted; septfoil footprint; pits in columns, the very narrow geometric strapwork, without outlines, forms pentagonal panels on the sides and kite-shaped on the tonsured crown; the crown strapwork resembles a six-spoked wheel; D *c.*20mm H20mm. *South East Dorset.*

91. Polygonal footprint, circumferential basal plain band with one groove, pits in columns, faceted sides and crown; geometric strapwork without outlines forms pentagonal and hexagonal panels on the sides and pentagonal on a pierced tonsured crown; the crown strapwork resembles a nine-petalled fleuret, D15.5mm H12mm. *Kent.*

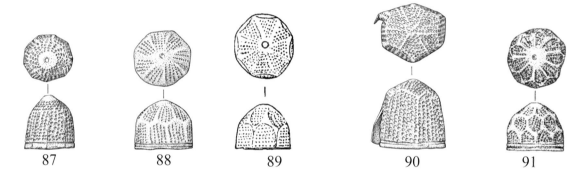

87   88   89   90   91

Domed thimbles *c.*1400 – *c.*1500

Copper-alloy domed thimbles ascribed as *c.*1400 – *c.*1500 were made by either casting, hammering sheet or, according to Holmes 1985, from *c.*1450, sheeting with longitudinal and horizontal soldered seams. The latter thimbles were presumably composite two-piece, of which no complete example has been noted during this present study, though a detached crown is perhaps from such a thimble (Fig. 14). Most are considerably larger and more robust than the aforesaid small skeps though this same name is frequently used. Oblique bases seem uncommon though one has such a feature (No. 114). Sides may be straighter, and crowns totally pitted or tonsured. Pits, minute or small, are circular, drilled or punched, and on the sides primarily configured in left-hand spirals, or more rarely right-hand (the latter are virtually impossible to differentiate from mid to late16th-century domed thimbles), or columns on the sides and concentric circles on crowns. As the 15th century progressed, use of pits in left-hand spirals increased until about the middle of the 16th century (see below). All configurations of pits may end at the start of a tonsure or extend over the whole of the crown. Circumferential basal plain bands are typical, and frequently engraved with circumferential single or double grooves. As mentioned above, one or more similar grooves separating side pits from the tonsure or open-top seem uncommon in the known record (Nos 81, 300-302 and Fig. 1 in Archaeological Small Finds Report: 0009.01, 2014, *A Medieval Sewing-Thimble From Dolbenmaen, Gwynedd*). Other decoration is seemingly uncommon; notwithstanding, three have simple engraving (Nos 105-106, 117), while tonsured crowns with openwork designs are becoming more apparent in the known record, three of which are noted (Nos 118-120). An openwork crown example was found in an archaeologically secure *c.*1450 – *c.*1500 context in Amsterdam (Langedijk and Boon 1999, ill. 57, cat. 22); cf pp 49 in De Smet 1992 also dated at *c.*1450 – *c.*1500 and found near Oudenburg, Flanders, Belgium. Fig. 71 in Isbister 2010 is classified as probably Burn's Type II (see below), therefore mid-16th century, an attribution refuted by the two former examples.

Although some of the *c.*1400 – *c.*1500 domed thimbles may have been produced in England, most are probably imports from Nuremberg or other European manufactories. Makers' marks are absent on these domed thimbles and both cast and hammered forms may feature small notches and/or small square indentations in or just above the basal rim (Nos 92, 106). As previously mentioned, this study revealed no silver domed-thimbles confidently confirmed as from the Middle Ages. Domed thimbles of this period, and later, as stated earlier, occasionally are found retaining a metal sleeve that frequently appears to be another thimble stored inside (Nos 94, 115).

A possible unfinished sheet copper-alloy domed thimble of about this date, a detectorist retrieved from a medieval midden uncovered during a pipeline excavation: it is completely flat, lacking any obvious trauma marks indicating squashing, 19mm diameter, with a left-hand spiral of drilled pits ending in a tonsure (Fig. 12). If formed into a domed crown of a composite two-piece thimble it would be a large specimen – conversely, hammering into a domed thimble would make it quite small. The documented and pictorial record has led us to believe that pits were applied to medieval and early post-medieval hammered domed thimbles after shaping. The aforesaid discovery suggests that, alternatively, pitting may have happened before hammering, as sometimes occurred with crowns of English mid-17th-century composite sheet thimbles.

Domed thimbles *c.*1400 – *c.*1500

All are possibly from Nuremberg. With or without circumferential plain bands and engraved grooves; unless specified otherwise, all are cast copper-alloy with probable drilled pits; and undecorated.

92. Two notches in basal rim suggests cast though a longitudinal partial pseudo scarfed seam perhaps indicates a split caused by insufficient annealing, therefore hammered; a circumferential basal narrow plain band with one groove, pits in columns on the lower two thirds of the sides and concentric circles on the upper third and the crown, D22.3mm H24.2mm. *South West Wiltshire.*

93. Uncertain whether cast or hammered, a circumferential basal narrow plain band with one groove, pits in columns on the lower two thirds of the sides and concentric circles on the upper third and the crown, D19.5mm H23mm. PAS LIN-ADB0B3. *Lincolnshire.*

94. Probably hammered, a small split in basal rim and slightly distorted, a circumferential basal plain band with two grooves, pits in columns on the lower two thirds of the sides and concentric circles on the upper third and crown, D19mm H20mm. An internal sleeve is possibly another thimble. *Berkshire.*

95. A circumferential basal wide plain band with two grooves, pits in columns on the lower two thirds of the sides and concentric circles on the upper third and crown, D21mm H20mm. PAS LIN-1556B7. *Lincolnshire.*

96. Two oblique grooves in the basal side suggest hammered; a circumferential basal wide plain band with one groove, pits in columns on the sides and concentric circles on the crown, D14mm H17mm. PAS LIN-004E41. *Lincolnshire.*

97. A circumferential basal plain band, a continuous left-hand spiral of pits on the sides and crown up to a trefoil-shaped tonsure, D21mm H21.8mm. *South Somerset.*

98. Possibly hammered, a small split in the rim, a circumferential basal plain band, a continuous left-hand spiral of pits on the sides and crown up to a tonsure pierced off-centre, D21mm H23mm. PAS SUR-D26BE0. *West Berkshire.*

99. Possibly hammered, a small split in the rim, a circumferential basal plain band, a continuous left-hand spiral of pits on the sides and crown up to a trefoil-shaped tonsure, D20mm H24.5mm. *South West Wiltshire.*

100. Four basal equidistant notches, a circumferential basal plain band, a continuous left-hand spiral of pits on the sides and flat crown up to a tonsure, D25mm H20.5mm. PAS HAMP-833852. *Hampshire.*

101. A circumferential basal plain band, a continuous left-hand spiral of pits on the sides and crown up to a tonsure, D19.5mm H19mm. *South Gloucestershire.*

102. Hammered; insufficient annealing possibly caused a split in the side which runs up to and slightly over the crown, the overlapped metal forms a pseudo unsoldered scarfed seam; a circumferential basal plain band with one groove, a continuous left-hand spiral of pits on the sides and crown; D21mm H17.4mm. *South West Dorset.*

103. Hammered, a circumferential basal plain band with two grooves, a continuous left-hand spiral of pits on the sides and crown up to a tonsure with a centring pit, D20mm H16mm. *South Somerset.*

104. A circumferential basal plain band with two grooves, a continuous left-hand spiral of pits on the sides and crown, D19mm H23mm. *South West Dorset.*

105. Possibly hammered; slightly distorted, insufficient annealing possibly caused a small split in the side, the overlapped metal forms a pseudo unsoldered scarfed seam; a circumferential basal plain band with one groove, a continuous left-hand spiral of pits on the sides and crown up to a tonsure with an engraved square, D22.04mm H13.72mm. PAS SUSS-D8E5F2. *East Sussex.*

106. Hammered; the basal rim has three small splits, probably due to insufficient annealing; a circumferential basal plain band with one groove punched with three small square indentations; a continuous left-hand spiral of punched circular pits on the sides and crown, the spiral of pits is interrupted by a deeply engraved groove spiralling left-hand from the basal groove up to the crown where it forms a tonsured teat; D23mm H24mm. *South West Wiltshire.*

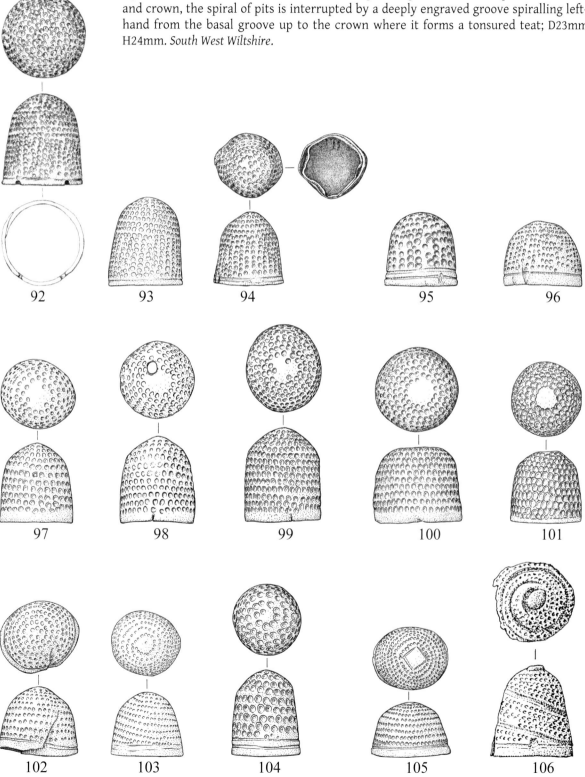

92 93 94 95 96
97 98 99 100 101
102 103 104 105 106

107. Hammered; a circumferential basal plain band, a continuous left-hand spiral of probably punched circular pits on the sides and crown, D17.5mm H15mm. *River Thames foreshore, London.*

108. Hammered, two splits in sides and slightly distorted; a circumferential basal plain band, a continuous left-hand spiral of probably punched circular pits on the sides and crown, D15.5mm H15.5mm. *Billingsgate flytip, London.*

109. Possibly hammered, a circumferential basal plain band, a continuous left-hand spiral of punched circular pits on the sides and crown up to a pierced tonsure, D15mm H19mm. *River Thames foreshore, London.*

110. Possibly hammered, a circumferential basal plain band, a continuous left-hand spiral of punched circular pits on the sides and crown up to a tonsure, D19mm H17mm. *South Somerset.*

111. Possibly hammered, a circumferential basal plain band with one faint groove, a continuous left-hand spiral of punched circular pits on the sides and crown up to a tonsure, D17mm H19mm. *River Thames foreshore, London.*

112. Possibly hammered, a circumferential basal plain band with one faint groove, a continuous left-hand spiral of punched oval/circular pits on the sides and crown up to a tonsure, D14mm H17.8mm. *River Thames foreshore, London.*

113. Hammered, a circumferential plain band with one faint groove, a continuous left-hand spiral of punched circular pits on the sides and slightly conical crown, D12mm H10mm. UKDFD 13102. *Staffordshire.*

114. Oblique base, a circumferential basal plain band with one groove, a continuous left-hand spiral of pits on the sides and crown up to a tonsure, D18mm H18mm. *Hampshire.*

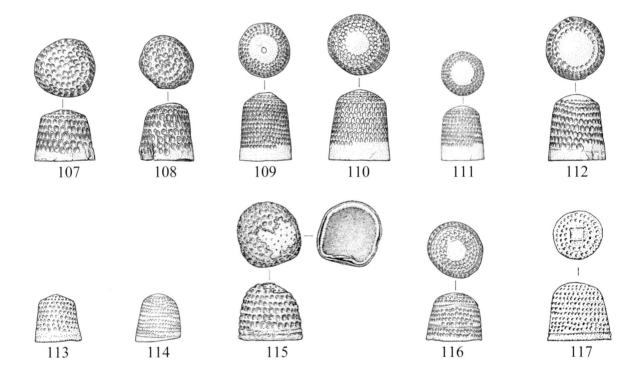

| 107 | 108 | 109 | 110 | 111 | 112 |

| 113 | 114 | 115 | 116 | 117 |

115. A section of crown broken off and distorted, a circumferential basal plain band with two grooves and a median ridge, a continuous left-hand spiral of pits on the sides and crown, D17.8mm H15mm. An internal sleeve appears to be another thimble with small circular pits evident. *Berkshire.*

116. Hammered, a circumferential basal plain band, the sides have two deep grooves that interrupt a left-hand spiral of probably punched circular pits, four concentric circles of similar pits on the crown up to a tonsure; D16.5mm H14mm. *West Buckinghamshire.*

117. A circumferential basal plain band with one groove, a continuous left-hand spiral of pits on the sides and crown up to a tonsure with an engraved square, D16.5mm H14mm. *Norfolk.*

Domed openwork thimbles *c*.1450 – *c*.1500

All are possibly from Nuremberg. All are probably cast copper-alloy with circumferential plain bands, possibly drilled pits and openwork decoration.

118. A circumferential basal plain band, a left-hand spiral of pits; a tonsured crown with openwork – four disconnected slots forming a saltire with a trefoil in each segment; D16.5mm H17mm. *South West Dorset.*

119. A circumferential basal plain band, a left-hand spiral of pits; a tonsured crown with openwork – three connected slots forming a tribrach motif with a heart in each segment; D15.3mm H19.5mm. *Wiltshire.*

120. A circumferential basal plain band, a left-hand spiral of pits; a tonsured crown with openwork – three disconnected slots forming a tribrach motif with a trefoil in each segment; D17mm H21mm. *South Somerset.*

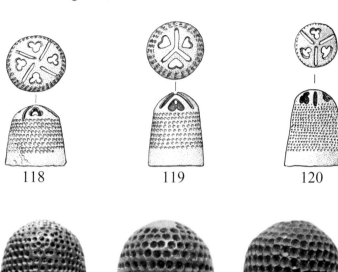

118 119 120

Figure 12. Possible unfinished domed sheet copper-alloy thimble *c*.1400 – *c*.1500. *Lincolnshire.* Note flatness, lack of trauma marks and left-hand spiral of drilled pits. Photo copyright and reproduced courtesy of Adam Staples.

Figure 13. Domed copper-alloy thimbles *c*.1400 – *c*.1500.

Figure 14. Detached crown, from a possible c.mid-15th-century domed composite two-piece hammered sheet copper-alloy thimble with soldered seams. *Wiltshire.*

Figure 15. Domed cast copper-alloy thimble with possible linen sleeve c.15th-century. *South Lincolnshire.* Photo copyright © and reproduced courtesy of Adam Staples.

Domed thimbles *c.*16th – *c.* mid-17th century

Sixteenth-century copper-alloy domed thimbles were predominantly cast until c.1530, being succeeded by hammered-sheet, though casting persisted on a lesser scale (Holmes 1988). As mentioned above, Nuremberg thimble-makers were incorporated into the Guild of Coppersmiths in 1494 after which they had to cast their own thimbles. Those cast lack possible mould spike-holes in the crown, and also absent are basal notches, wedges or oblique lines, therefore other methods of securing in the mould and the lathe must have been used.

Many early 16th-century cast or hammered copper-alloy domed thimbles look much the same as their immediate antecedents, being fairly large but often with flatter crowns. Interestingly, Jost Amman's 1539-91 engraving of a Nuremberg thimble-maker's workshop depicts domed thimbles with seemingly pronounced basal rims (Fig. 20). Apart from one found too late for cataloguing herein (PAS WILT-C48651), this present study failed to reveal such a feature on surviving specimens ascribed as late medieval or early post-medieval; cf ill. 9, cat. 84, in Langedijk and Boon 1999, which has a slight basal rim, formed after the engraving of a circumferential groove. Nonetheless, such a groove or grooves often create a noticeable shallow rim, as with several herein (Nos 127, 133-135, 143, 171-172); moreover, two composite thimbles feature well-defined rims (Nos 136, 147).

Initially, pits were circular, drilled or punched, however, around the middle of the 16th century additional shapes appeared (see above). Early to mid-16th-century copper-alloy domed thimbles archaeologically excavated in Amsterdam are configured in spirals, mainly left-hand and to a lesser extent right-hand: as far as this study show, the latter configuration predominates on these thimbles found by detectorists in Britain. This means it is difficult or impossible to ascribe them as early or mid-16th century, a problem exacerbated further as from about the middle of the 16th century right-hand spirals prevailed. Either spiral configuration may extend uninterrupted over the crown or stop short at a tonsure, the latter characteristic said to have been phased out c.1650 (Holmes 1985) though this is contentious (see below). One or two circumferential basal engraved grooves, or punched dot bands, is normal, and other decoration is recorded herein (Nos 121, 137-150, 168, 175-181, 186-196). As mentioned above, from c.1520 Nuremberg thimble-makers (and journeymen and contractors, too) started to punch their respective marks on copper-alloy domed and ring-type thimbles; and on domed forms again such marks are normally at the start of the spiral, but occasionally seen further around the base or on or above the circumferential basal groove or grooves (Nos 151-174, 179-185, 194-196). On copper-alloy domed thimbles, single makers' marks appear to be restricted to those hammered and double marks on cast.

Three possibly hammered copper-alloy domed thimbles have concave sides (Nos 132, 173-174), an unusual profile on domed thimbles found in Britain but occasionally evident on ring-types (see above). One has two anomalous marks stamped away from the start of the spiral (No. 173) – the maker's and perhaps a journeyman's or contractor's; a second thimble is marked at the start of the spiral (No. 174) while the third is unmarked (No. 132). A thimble of this kind is shown on the Entner family epitaph (see below), and they are recorded in Germany, cf *Nürnberger Fingerhüte* 2014 pp 30, 34. Another shape, but probably cast, seemingly uncommon in Britain, but not so in Germany and the Netherlands, is very squat with a shallow-domed crown (Nos 123, 126-127), cf *Nürnberger Fingerhüte* 2014 pp 30-31, 34.

Early post-medieval silver domed-thimbles are seemingly rare survivals; five herein are notable: one is probably hammered sheet and ascribed as 15th- early 16th-century therefore perhaps late medieval, with a possible separately soldered basal rim, which if correct, means composite two-piece construction (No. 136); another is ascribed as late 15th century (No. 138) (after Mills 1999 No. NM.67), a third and a fourth are composite two-piece (Nos 148-149) while a fifth is composite three-piece (No. 150).

Around 1534, it is thought that one Paracelsus, a notable physician, lodged with Nuremberg thimble-maker Georg Entner (aka Endtner), and apart from medical matters, in a back room there he experimented in reducing pure zinc from calamine soil. Dr Paracelsus was successful and thereafter the availability of pure zinc allowed a brass alloy of a higher malleable quality from which thin sheets were hammered into rolls – Greif 1986, and Eigmüller & Lauterbach 2014. This metal glistened like gold and its improved malleability and thin gauge facilitated the hammering process responsible for the exquisite domed thimbles still found in Britain and elsewhere to this day. This invention meant Nuremberg thimble-makers were allowed to set up their own guild and casting became obsolete (Greif 1986). Sixteenth-century Nuremberg thimbles were exported over much of the then known world but according to Greif 1986, paradoxically none had been found in Nuremberg itself. However, it appears that several have turned up in the city and are now in Museum I22I20I18I Kühnertsgasse, Nuremberg.

As explained above, Nuremberg thimble-makers amalgamated with the Guild of Coppersmiths c.1494 and subsequently cast their own thimble cups, i.e. domes (Greif 1986). The earliest known date of a thimble-maker in Nuremberg is 1373, one Sebastian Prawn. During the 16th century Nuremberg had more than 90 master thimble-makers. Some 400 or more family names of thimble-makers are recorded whom respectively practised between the 14th and 18th centuries. Apart from the aforesaid Sebastian Prawn and Georg Entner, among others, their respective surnames are: Alfeld, Amman, Apel, Beck, Bischoff, Dresher, Ehe, Ellenbach, Entl (possibly aka Entner), Grabner, Gruener, Hubner, Kessler, Lang, Leyss, Lynen, Mathes, Merz, Muehlhorfer or Muehldorfer, Prym, Reuter, Rosenberger, Schleicher, Schmidt, Schreiner, Schuster, Tober, Ulschos, Urban, Vogel, Weigal, Welcher, Windl and Wolf (Greif 1986). Unfortunately, the Nuremberg masters' lists, including thimble-makers, were lost c.1571 (the reason is unclear).

Between 1425-6 and c.1806 names of other thimble-makers were recorded in the *Mendelschen Institute Housebook II* and also the *Landauer Foundation Memorial Book I*, the latter a second inventory used from the late 15th century until c.1806, namely: Hanns Franck (1649-?), Georg Henla (1569-1640), Wolfgang Laim (1549-1621), Ving [...] (c.1414), Martin Winderlein (1557-1627) and Nicolaus Zeittenburger, a journeyman (1596-1667).

With the exception of two marks attributed to the Entner family – a standing duck facing left and a crown – any particular mark is impossible to couple with its maker. The 1557 Entner family bronze epitaph in St Johannis Cemetery, Nuremberg shows such a duck between two crowns. Apparently, Entner's copper-alloy thimbles were stamped with the duck and the crown on those of precious metal; notwithstanding, copper-alloy domed and ring-type thimbles with a crown maker's mark are catalogued here (Nos. 40-41, 167). Similar bronze epitaphs for thimble-making families are found in Nuremberg, e.g. St Johannis Cemetery – 1580 Hans Tober, which shows five domed thimbles and a chalice supported by two angels; 1590 Mathes Kessler, which depicts two domed thimbles, one each side of a cooking vessel; St Rochus Cemetery – 1598 Georg Ehe, which has three domed thimbles above a putto; 1622 Martin Winderlein, which shows three domed thimbles on a shield. Whether any of these latter symbols represent the respective family marks is uncertain. Additional to a maker's mark, Nuremberg thimbles, and other metal items too, were apparently sometimes stamped with a Nuremberg eagle or a letter N (Greif 1986). Such marks were not noted during this present study.

Circa 1500 Nuremberg's Hans Grabner invented a knurling wheel with a single row of teeth, used in conjunction with a lathe, for impressing circular pits on the sides of his thimbles, but the Nuremberg Court prohibited its use, therefore hand punching continued as the primary method (Greif 1986). Holmes 1985 states that Garterer, writing in 1784, indicates pits on Nuremberg thimbles were still being hand punched and may have contributed to the demise of the industry in Nuremberg. In November 1572 the Nuremberg Thimble-makers' Guild complained to Nuremberg Court about a mechanical technique for deep drawing and grooving thimbles devised by master thimble-maker Joerg Entner. The Court banned Entner's new manufactory method as it would disadvantage other Nuremberg thimble-makers (Greif 1986).

Before 1573 Joerg Entner and his brother Hans started producing domed thimbles but again the Court thwarted Joerg due to the Thimble-makers' Guild complaining. According to the Court decree, no thimble-maker was permitted to make deep drawn, i.e. hammered, or soldered iron thimbles. We can infer that the latter were either composite two-piece domed or ring-types, or both, with soldered seams. In January 1589 another prominent Nuremberg thimble-maker, the aforesaid Hans Tober, also applied to produce iron thimbles and indeed did gain permission from the Court, however, after an objection by the Thimble-makers' Guild, the Court rescinded its approval. Tober reapplied in October 1590, a request again turned down. Apparently, iron thimbles were already being made outside of Nuremberg (whereabouts is unclear) before Entner and Tober's applications, a fact that failed to influence favourably the Nuremberg Thimble-makers' Guild and Court.

A c.19th- – c.20th-century mechanically knurled malleable iron/steel example, with a longitudinal soldered butt-seamed sheet copper-alloy sleeve, has an unknown provenance though is not from the soil (Fig. 16). Two others herein (Figs 16-17) are ascribed the same date and are from rural dispositions. The present writer has seen other excavated just about identifiable malleable iron/ steel domed thimbles, all virtually solid rust, of uncertain age. Curiously, these thimbles seem to be unrecorded from the River Thames foreshore in London, a place where they ought to survive in reasonable condition.

Burn 2001 classified possible Nuremberg-made decorated domed thimbles, both cast and hammered, into four types: Type I early 16th century, Type II mid-16th century, Type III late 16th century and Type IV early 17th century. This chronological morphology, which is based on shape and decoration, is confusing and does not necessarily square with the archaeological evidence, e.g. from Amsterdam (Langedijk and Boon 1999), and Croatia (Mileusnic 2004). Holmes 1988, who did not have the benefit of later archaeological evidence, ascribes Burn's Type I to 1550 – 1620, although the former date now antecedes 1545 (see below).

Burn's four hammered types have punched circular pits configured in right- or left-hand spirals. Those cast have thicker sides, and pits and their configuration and decoration may be similar as found on hammered specimens, though frequently these features are very different. It can be difficult to differentiate Burn's Types I – IV; both hammered or cast are decorated, frequently ornately, individually punched or applied under pressure using a rolling die and a lathe. These four types may exhibit white-metal or black coating. A further style of possible Nuremberg-made hammered sheet domed thimble is unmentioned by Burn's: generally these are tall, slim and undecorated other than one or two circumferential basal plain bands and engraved grooves; makers' marks are normal. These aforesaid anomalies influenced the present writer to simplify Burn's typology as below.

Read Type I hammered sheet copper-alloy possible Nuremberg-made domed thimbles may be either short or tall with pointed crowns (Nos 175-181) and usually have circumferential upper and basal plain bands with single or double engraved grooves. Punched circular, square/rectangular/sub-rectangular or reversed D-shaped pits spiral right-hand in the wider interstices of the sides and circular pits may continue uninterrupted over the pointed crowns or crowns may have separate right-hand spirals. An exceptional example here came from the River Thames foreshore, London and has punched pits shaped as six-pointed stars (No. 181); cf De Smet A, 1992 for a 1598 silver specimen with both circular and cross-shaped pits. Common on many is one or two circumferential basal bands of punched and engraved decoration such as crescents, cross-hatching or rectangles. Makers' marks are present on some (Nos. 179-181). A domed thimble of this kind with a maker's mark is described as being English by McConnel 1991, however, here it is considered as possibly from Nuremberg, and there appears to be no evidence whatsoever to support the suggestion that sheet-metal types were made from two pieces soldered together.

A typical specimen was recovered in 1976 from of a mid-16th-century Portuguese vessel wrecked off the Seychelles (Blake W and Green J, 1986). This mid-16th-century date means Burn's Type I was still being used, a plausible scenario, or at that time remained in production.

In 1967 the wreck of a Venetian ship discovered close to the island of Gnalić, Croatia, nowadays Biograd, and four sizes of Burn's Type I thimbles, many of which were salvaged, formed part of her cargo. As two of her recovered canons bear the date 1582 it confirms the vessel sailed to Gnalić after that year. Research by marine archaeologists revealed that the *Gagiana,* a Venetian ship, disappeared in 1583 near Gnalić; this is possibly the same vessel as the wreck (Mileusnic 2004). If correct, it means that Burn's Type I thimbles were still being produced in the late 16th century, therefore either the ship's early 16th-century attribution is doubtful or the longevity of these thimbles extended well towards 1600. That these distinctive domed thimbles always have pits in right-hand spirals and pits sometimes other than circular, the latter a diagnostic feature after about the mid-16th century, it appears to support the Gnalić evidence. Interestingly, the *Mary Rose* surrendered a Burn's Type I thimble punched with right-hand spirals of circular pits on both its crown and sides. The configuration of the spirals suggests an attribution of about the last half of the 16th century while the circular pits, before 1550, the latter date supported by the 1545 sinking of the *Mary Rose.*

Consideration of all the aforesaid evidence means Holmes' 1550 – 1620 attribution for Burn's Type I can be confidently revised as anteceding 1545. However, makers' marks started to be used from *c.*1520 and as the Burn's Type I in McConnel 1991 has a maker's mark, as have others found in Amsterdam, it implies Type I possibly could be ascribed as early as *c.*1520. This reinforces Burn's early 16th-century attribution for Type I. Regrettably, neither Holmes nor Burn explain how they arrived at their dating and until fresh reliable archaeological evidence comes to light, we can only speculate on precisely when these probable Nuremberg domed thimbles were first made.

Read Type II hammered sheet copper-alloy domed thimbles are probably from Nuremberg and have rounded crowns, punched circular pits configured in continuous right-hand spirals on the sides and crowns though crowns may have concentric circles; circumferential basal plain bands engraved with one or more grooves is normal as are makers' marks, while decoration is absent (Nos 182-185).

33

Figure 16. Domed malleable iron/steel thimble with copper-alloy sleeve *c.* late post-medieval. Private collection.

Figure 17. Domed malleable iron/steel thimble with copper-alloy sleeve *c.* late post-medieval. *Buckinghamshire.*

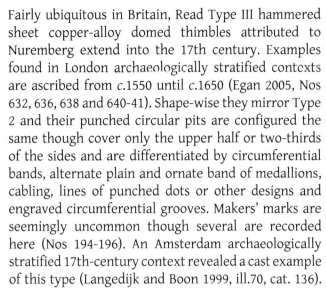

Figure 18. Domed malleable iron/steel thimble *c.* late post-medieval. *East Devon.*

Fairly ubiquitous in Britain, Read Type III hammered sheet copper-alloy domed thimbles attributed to Nuremberg extend into the 17th century. Examples found in London archaeologically stratified contexts are ascribed from *c.*1550 until *c.*1650 (Egan 2005, Nos 632, 636, 638 and 640-41). Shape-wise they mirror Type 2 and their punched circular pits are configured the same though cover only the upper half or two-thirds of the sides and are differentiated by circumferential bands, alternate plain and ornate band of medallions, cabling, lines of punched dots or other designs and engraved circumferential grooves. Makers' marks are seemingly uncommon though several are recorded here (Nos 194-196). An Amsterdam archaeologically stratified 17th-century context revealed a cast example of this type (Langedijk and Boon 1999, ill.70, cat. 136). Three domed thimbles of this type are depicted on the aforesaid Hans Tober 1580 epitaph.

During the early post-medieval period, other styles of domed thimble appeared, either cast, hammered or composite sheet copper-alloy or silver. For detectorists, British depositions have revealed several varieties, either with minimal or ornate decoration (137-150). Continental thimble-makers are probably responsible for some, though without doubt others are English. Apparently still discovered in Northern Spain and Southern France are cast copper-alloy domed thimbles of a type seemingly uncommon as detecting finds in Britain: typically they feature decorated crowns, and geometric linear strapwork, without engraved outlines, punched with multiple fleurs-de-lis (Nos 139, 143). The latter example bears a shield, perhaps addorsed with a second shield, each with three fleurs-de-lis. From the late 12th century the traditional arms of France were 'Azure, a semis of fleurs-de-lis or', i.e. golden fleurs-de-lis strewn liberally on a blue field. In 1376 France's King Charles V changed his arms to 'Azure, three fleurs-de-lis or', i.e. three fleurs-de-lis configured two surmounting one. These variations of the French arms are respectively described as 'France Ancient' and 'France Modern'. Use of the fleur-de-lis symbol suggests these thimbles are French-made and those bearing multiple fleur-de-lis could be as early as 12th century while others with only three may date from 1376; however, Isbister 2002 ascribes them as *c.*16th century.

Domed thimbles *c.*1500 – *c.*1600

All are possibly from Nuremberg. With or without circumferential plain bands and engraved grooves; unless specified otherwise, all are cast copper-alloy with drilled pits, undecorated and without makers' marks.

121. Hammered, bell-shaped, split in side; two circumferential plain bands, one basal and the other midway; a continuous right-hand spiral of punched circular pits on the sides and crown up to a tonsure; several crudely engraved grooves spiral left-hand between the basal and middle plain bands, D16mm H19mm. *River Thames foreshore, London.*

122. A circumferential basal plain band, a continuous right-hand spiral of pits on the sides and crown, D17mm H17.5mm. *South West Wiltshire.*

123. Fairly straight sides, a continuous right-hand spiral of pits on the sides and crown, D17.5mm H13.8mm. *Gwynedd, Wales.*

124. Fairly straight sides, a continuous right-hand spiral of pits on the sides and crown, D19.5mm H17.8mm. *South Lincolnshire.*

125. Bell-shaped, circumferential upper and basal plain bands, a right-hand spiral of punched circular pits on the sides and a separate spiral of punched triangular pits on the crown, D21mm H23mm. *South East Dorset.*

126. Straight sides, a circumferential basal plain band with one groove, a continuous right-hand spiral of drilled pits on the sides and crown, D16mm H13.8mm. *South Lincolnshire.*

127. Straight sides, a circumferential basal plain band with one deep groove creating a rim, a continuous right-hand spiral of punched oval pits on the sides and crown, D16mm H14mm. *South Lincolnshire.*

128. Possibly hammered, split in side, a circumferential basal plain band with one groove, a continuous right-hand spiral of punched oval pits on the sides and crown, D18mm H20mm. *North Dorset.*

129 A circumferential basal plain band with one groove, a continuous right-hand spiral of punched reversed D-shaped pits on the sides and crown, D19.5mm H20mm. *South Somerset.*

130. Possibly hammered, slightly distorted, a circumferential basal plain band with one groove; a continuous right-hand spiral of pits on the sides and crown, the spiral midway is deeply grooved which suggests possible application using a single knurling wheel, D19.5mm H20mm. *Berkshire.*

131. Hammered, a circumferential basal plain band with two grooves, a continuous right-hand spiral of punched triangular pits on the sides and crown up to a tonsure, D18.5mm H22mm. PAS SWYOR-B87F57. *South West Yorkshire.*

132. Possibly hammered; concave sides with a seemingly soldered scarfed seam in the basal rim, probably a repaired split caused by insufficient annealing; a circumferential basal plain band with two grooves, a continuous right-hand spiral of pits on the sides and crown, D18.5mm H16.8mm. *River Thames foreshore, London.*

133. Circumferential upper and basal plain bands, each with three grooves, a right-hand spiral of pits on the sides and a separate right-hand spiral of pits on the crown, D16mm H19.5mm. *River Thames foreshore, London.*

134. A circumferential basal plain band with two deep grooves and three distinct ridges, the lower creating a rim, a right-hand spiral of punched circular pits on the sides, the crown has a circumferential plain band with two engraved grooves and a left-hand spiral of punched circular pits, D19mm H24mm. *Billingsgate fly tip, London.*

135. Fairly straight sides, a circumferential basal plain band with two faint grooves, the lower creating a rim; concentric circles of pits on the sides and crown up to a tonsure, D15mm H19.4mm. *River Thames foreshore, London.*

136. Silver, sheet, possibly composite, squashed; concentric circles of pits on sides and crown, an indistinct punched mark in centre of the crown; a pronounced rim is possibly separately soldered, D24mm H18mm. Perhaps late medieval. PAS IOW-C61748, 2008 T133. *Isle of Wight.*

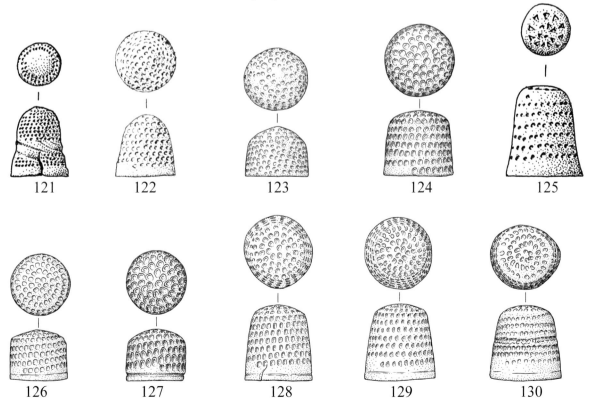

121   122   123   124   125

126   127   128   129   130

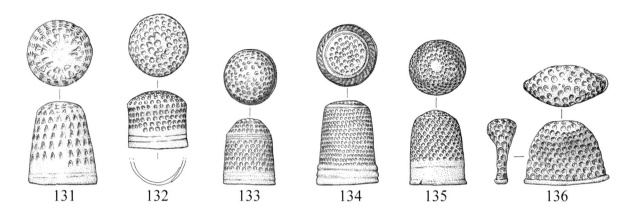

131   132   133   134   135   136

Domed thimbles *c*.1500 – *c*.1600

From various, some uncertain, European manufactories. With or without circumferential plain bands and engraved grooves; unless specified otherwise, all are cast copper-alloy with punched pits, decorated with engraving and/or punchwork and without makers' marks.

137. Possibly from Nuremberg, oblique base, white-metal coated, a circumferential basal plain band, a continuous right-hand spiral of circular pits alternating with continuous linear and curvilinear faint grooves on the sides and crown culminating centrally with seven annulets forming a fleuret; D14.2mm H13mm. *West Buckinghamshire.*

138. Possibly French, silver-gilt, possibly cast, a circumferential basal plain band with one groove, leaves and a medieval French blackletter inscription **+ MA JO IE** meaning **MY JOY**; circular pits configured either in a left-hand spiral or concentric circles; decoration and inscription possibly nielloed, dimensions unknown. After Mills 1999. *River Thames foreshore, London.*

139. Probably French, ragged basal rim; columns of circular pits on the sides, geometric strapwork without outlines comprising circumferential upper, basal and median plain bands and a vertical plain band on the sides, the latter with six random indistinct marks; the tonsured crown has a quatrefoil within two concentric circles, the inner beaded and the outer linear; D19mm H21.5mm. *South West Dorset.*

140. Possibly from Nuremberg, pointed crown, circumferential upper and basal plain bands, columns of circular pits on the sides, a tonsured crown with a quatrefoil formed from four lozenges of circular pits, D17mm H22mm. *South West Lincolnshire.*

141. Possibly from Nuremberg; circumferential upper and basal plain bands, the basal with one groove; columns of alternate circular pits and vertical lines on the sides; the crown has an equal-armed cross in a circle, the interstices are filled with lines of circular pits, D15mm H19mm. *South Somerset.*

142. Probably from Nuremberg, a circumferential basal plain band with one groove, drilled pits in concentric circles on the sides, a tonsured crown with four large voided roundels, D15.5mm H21.5mm. PAS LON-1A40F7. *River Thames foreshore, London.*

143. French; circumferential upper, median and basal plain bands, each with two grooves, the basal grooves are flanked with a ridge each side creating a rim; columns of circular pits on the sides; the lower interstice of a vertical plain band on the side bears an adaptation of the arms of France modern – a shield containing three fleur-de-lis – each within a lozenge, the upper interstice has identical fleurs and lozenges though no shield; the crown has a central quatrefoil formed from four ovals within a raised roundel surrounded with similar fleurs within lozenges, and then a circle, D17mm H23mm. *South Lincolnshire.*

144. Possibly from Nuremberg, fairly straight sides divided into three circumferential bands separated by grooves, the wide basal band has dots forming an unintelligible inscription HO - PTER – TER; half of the wider median band has dots forming an arrow piercing a heart filled with pits, the other half has seven rows of pits; the upper band has three grooves and two ridges; the crown has pits outlining a Cross Moline, each arm of which has a median line of pits, D16.5mm H20mm. PAS IOW2010-1-481, *Isle of Wight.*

145. Possibly from Nuremberg, circumferential upper and basal plain bands; basal with three grooves, hatching between the centre two; concentric circles of pits on the sides and a plain panel with dots forming an arrow piercing a heart flanked each side with foliate; the crown has dots forming a cross with a stylised fleur in each angle, D12.5mm H17.3mm. *River Thames foreshore, London.*

146. Possibly from Nuremberg; circumferential upper and basal plain bands, each with three grooves separated by ridges; the basal lower two ridges and groove have repeating oblique dashes; concentric circles of drilled pits on the sides and separate concentric circles on the crown, D19.5mm H23mm. *Billingsgate fly tip, London.*

147. Possibly from Nuremberg or England, composite three-piece sheet, longitudinal and horizontal soldered butt seams; a separately soldered rim, concentric circles of drilled pits on the sides; the crown is unpitted and has an intaglio interpreted as – a (?) crowned heart over (?) water and an unintelligible inscription [?] IL MIAITI within a circle – suggesting this thimble had a secondary function as a seal matrix; traces of black coating on the sides, crown and inside (during the late medieval early post-medieval periods several varieties of crowned or flowering hearts were popular motifs, e.g. on brooches, seal matrices and finger-rings); D12mm H15.5mm. *Thames foreshore, London.*

148. Probably English, sheet silver, composite two-piece; distorted with sprung longitudinal and horizontal soldered seams; circumferential upper and basal plain bands, each with two grooves, the basal band has intermittent crosses; probable concentric circles of circular pits on the sides, a four-petalled flower within a circle on the crown, D23mm H20.07mm. PAS SUSS-048416, 2010 T288. *West Sussex.*

149. Probably English, sheet silver, composite two-piece with indeterminate longitudinal and horizontal soldered seams, circumferential upper and basal bands, the upper with two grooves, basal with three grooves and voided zigzags with transverse grooves; concentric circles of triangular pits on the sides, a Tudor rose on the crown; sporadic gilding, possibly anaerobic; D15.5mm H18.83mm. PAS LON-BB52BE, 2015 T745. *River Thames foreshore, Queenhithe, London.*

150. Possibly Dutch, sheet silver, composite three-piece; longitudinal lapped and scarfed and horizontal probably scarfed soldered seams; a circumferential basal plain band with a scalloped edge and a separate soldered hemispherical cross-section rim; above the basal band circumferential grooves divide the sides into four further differing width bands with: transverse grooves, repeating lozenges with saltires and pellets; transverse grooves, repoussé and engraved stylised tulips; the crown has a right-hand spiral of circular pits, D16mm H22.5mm. *(?) Norfolk.*

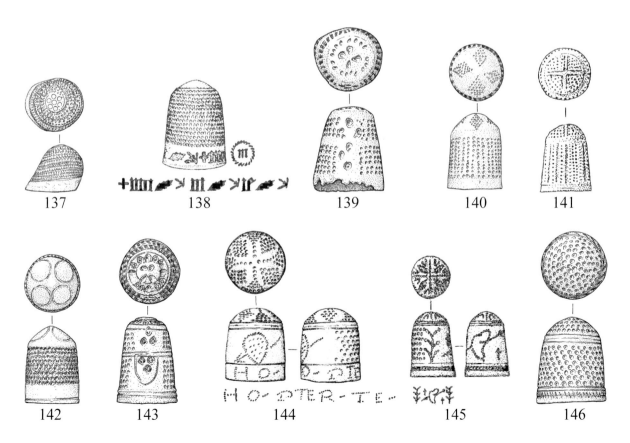

137   138   139   140   141

142   143   144   145   146

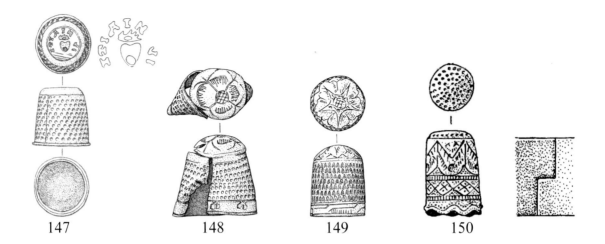

147   148   149   150

Domed thimbles *c*.1520 – *c*.1600

All are probably from Nuremberg. Unless specified otherwise, cast copper-alloy with punched pits, with or without circumferential plain bands and engraved grooves, with makers' marks, and undecorated.

151. A circumferential basal plain band, a continuous right-hand spiral of oval pits on the sides and crown up to a tonsure; maker's mark at start of spiral – cross outlined by four asymmetrical shapes; D21mm H21mm. *West Gloucestershire.*

152. A circumferential basal plain band with one groove, a continuous right-hand spiral of oval pits on the sides and crown; maker's mark at start of spiral – quatrefoil in a circular cartouche; D14mm H17mm. *River Thames foreshore, London.*

153. A circumferential basal plain band with one groove, a continuous right-hand spiral of oval pits on the sides and crown; maker's mark at start of spiral – quatrefoil in an asymmetrical cartouche; D14.5mm H18.2mm. *River Thames foreshore, London.*

154. A circumferential basal plain band with one groove, a continuous right-hand spiral of oval pits on the sides and crown; maker's mark – quatrefoil in a circular cartouche; D17mm H19.8mm. *South Somerset.*

155. A continuous right-hand spiral of oval pits on the sides and crown; maker's mark at start of spiral – chevron in hemispherical cartouche surmounted by two pellets; D14.5mm H18.2mm. *River Thames foreshore, London.*

156. A circumferential basal plain band with one groove, a continuous right-hand spiral of oval pits on the sides and crown; maker's mark away from start of spiral – indeterminate, vertical bar, 1 or capital I; D16.5mm H18.8mm. *Lincolnshire.*

157. A circumferential basal plain band with one groove, a continuous right-hand spiral of oval/circular pits on the sides and crown; maker's mark at start of spiral – indeterminate asymmetrical shape in an asymmetrical cartouche; D18.5mm H20mm. *River Thames foreshore, London.*

158. A circumferential basal plain band with one groove, a continuous right-hand spiral of oval pits on the sides and abraded crown; maker's mark at start of spiral – indeterminate, D19mm H20mm. *South West Wiltshire.*

159. A circumferential basal plain band with one groove, maker's mark at start of spiral – cross outlined by four pellets, D19mm H23mm. *River Thames foreshore, London.*

160. Possibly hammered, a circumferential basal plain band with one faint groove, a continuous right-hand spiral of oval pits on the sides and crown; maker's mark at start of spiral – two conjoined lozenges in a subrectangular cartouche, D18mm H20mm. *River Thames foreshore, London.*

161. Possibly hammered, distorted, a circumferential basal plain band with one groove, a continuous right-hand spiral of oval pits on the sides and crown; maker's mark at start of spiral – A in a shield-shaped cartouche; D20mm H21.5mm. *South Somerset.*

162. Possibly hammered, split in side; a circumferential basal plain band with one groove; a continuous right-hand spiral of pits, square on the sides and circular the crown; maker's mark away from start of spiral – saltire in a square cartouche; D20.09mm H18.97mm. PAS NLM-A9A121. *Norfolk.*

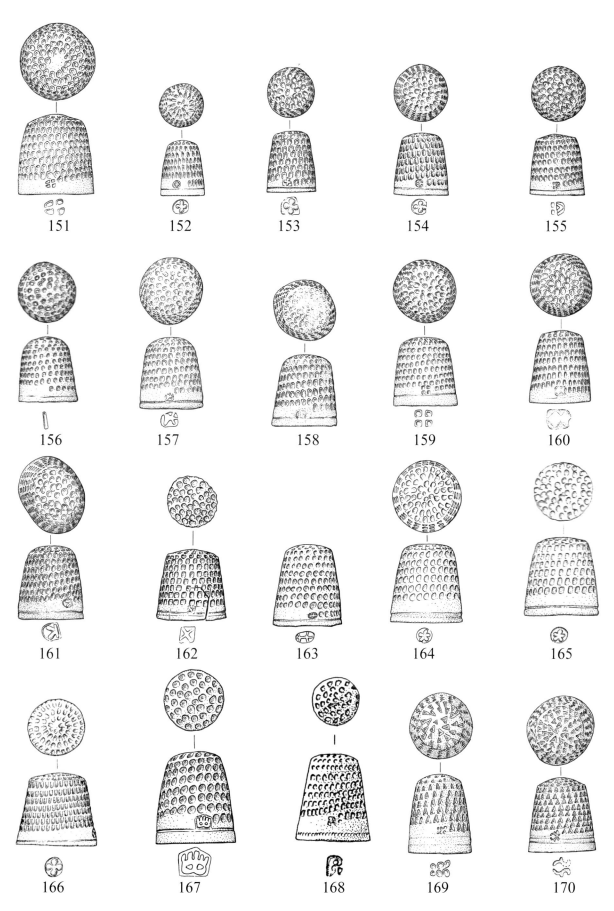

151   152   153   154   155

156   157   158   159   160

161   162   163   164   165

166   167   168   169   170

163. A circumferential basal plain band with one groove, a continuous right-hand spiral of D-shaped/oval pits on the sides and crown; maker's mark at start of spiral – bar with two oblique bars each side in an oval cartouche; D20mm H22mm. UKDFD 7885. *County Durham.*

164. A circumferential basal plain band with one deep groove, a continuous right-hand spiral of reversed D-shaped pits on the sides and crown; maker's mark at start of spiral – cinquefoil in a circular cartouche; D21.2mm H21.7mm. PAS HAMP-A3F9E1. *Hampshire.*

165. A circumferential basal plain band with one groove, a continuous right-hand spiral of oval pits on the sides and circular the crown; maker's mark at start of spiral – cinquefoil in circular cartouche; D20.5mm H21mm. *South Somerset.*

166. A circumferential basal plain band with one groove, a continuous right-hand spiral of elongated oval pits on the sides and crown; maker's mark at start of spiral – quatrefoil in a circular cartouche, 23.4mm H20mm. *South West Dorset.*

167. A circumferential basal plain band with one groove, a continuous right-hand spiral of drilled pits on the sides and crown; maker's mark at start of spiral – possibly a crown in a pentagonal cartouche; D19mm H24mm. *Kent.*

168. A circumferential basal plain band with a punched beaded band, a continuous right-hand spiral of oval pits on the sides and crown; maker's mark at start of spiral – R; D21.5mm H23mm. *Essex.*

169. A circumferential basal plain band with two grooves, a continuous right-hand spiral of triangular pits on the sides and crown; maker's mark at start of spiral – six oval/circular pits forming a leaf shape; D18.4mm H21. *South East Dorset.*

170. A circumferential basal plain band with two grooves, a continuous right-hand spiral of triangular pits on the sides and crown; maker's mark on the upper groove – two addorsed S-like scrolls; D19.5mm H21mm. *River Thames foreshore, London.*

171. A circumferential basal plain band with two grooves and two ridges creating a rim, a continuous right-hand spiral of circular pits on the sides and crown; maker's mark – shears in an oval cartouche, D15.5mm H21mm. *River Thames foreshore, London.*

172. A circumferential basal plain band with two deep grooves, the upper one wide, and two ridges, the lower creating a rim; concentric circles of triangular pits on the sides and crown; the wide band has four equidistant punched five-point stars, each with a central pellet; these may be purely decorative or maker's marks; D18mm H23mm. PAS NMS-F52502. *Norfolk.*

173. Possibly hammered, concave sides, a circumferential basal plain band with one groove, a continuous right-hand spiral of drilled pits on the sides and crown; two anomalous maker's marks away from start of spiral – cinquefoil formed from annulets and four pellets forming a lozenge; D20mm H15mm. *Buckinghamshire.*

174. Concave sides, a circumferential basal plain band with two grooves, the lower creating a rim, a continuous right-hand spiral of drilled pits on the sides and crown; maker's mark at start of spiral – three pellets forming a chevron; D17mm H14mm. *River Thames foreshore, London.*

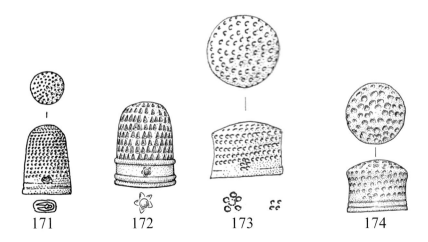

171   172   173   174

Domed thimbles *c.1520 – c.1650*

All are probably from Nuremberg. Probably cast copper-alloy with pointed crowns, punched pits, circumferential plain bands and engraved grooves and engraved decoration; unless specified otherwise, without makers' marks.

175. A circumferential upper plain band with two grooves, a basal band with four grooves and repeating curlicues, a right-hand spiral of rectangular pits on the sides and a separate similar spiral on the crown, D15.4mm H19mm. *River Thames foreshore, London.*

176. Circumferential upper and basal bands, the upper plain and basal with four grooves and two-strand interlace, a right-hand spiral of rectangular pits on sides and a separate similar spiral on the crown, D16.5mm H20mm. *South West Wiltshire.*

177. Slightly distorted, three grooves forming two bands, each with repeating annulets, and a plain band; a continuous spiral of circular/oval pits on the sides and crown, D20mm H23mm. *West Buckinghamshire.*

178. Section of crown broken off and slightly corroded, a circumferential upper plain band with one groove; a basal band with three grooves forming two bands, the wider with repeating cinquefoils in rectangles, a right-hand spiral of oval pits on sides and a separate similar spiral on the crown, a separate internal sleeve is possibly another thimble, D21.8mm H23mm. *West Buckinghamshire.*

179. Circumferential basal bands, two plain and one cabled; square pits in concentric circles on the sides and crown, maker's mark partly on the cabled band – a nine-pointed rowel or star in a circular cartouche, D16mm H17.4mm. *South Gloucestershire.*

180. Circumferential upper plain band with one groove; a basal plain band with three grooves forming four bands, one has repeating lozenges with a central pellet in rectangles; a right-hand spiral of drilled pits on sides and a separate similar spiral on the crown; maker's mark on the upper basal groove – comma with three oblique projections in an asymmetrical cartouche, D19mm H24mm. UKDFD 40226. *Norfolk.*

181. White-metal coated; a circumferential upper band of zigzags and pellets and a groove; the lower half of the sides has three decorated bands: the upper, geometric shapes and a groove each side; the middle, alternate foliate and animals, perhaps a coursing scene, within beaded borders; the basal, geometric shapes and one groove; the upper quarter of the sides and the crown have possible concentric circles of six-pointed star pits; two maker's marks are punched below the side pits – two tree- or mushroom-like shapes, each with three internal pellets; D19mm H25mm. *River Thames foreshore, London.*

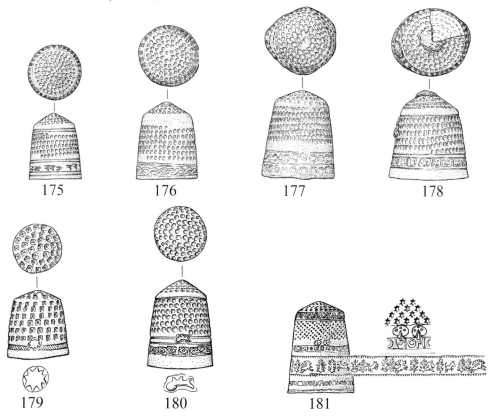

175   176   177   178

179   180   181

Domed thimbles *c*.1520 – *c*.1650

All are probably from Nuremberg. Hammered copper-alloy with punched pits, circumferential basal plain bands and engraved grooves, makers' marks and undecorated.

182. A circumferential basal plain band with one faint groove, a continuous right-hand spiral of rectangular pits on sides and crown; maker's mark away from start of spiral – two conjoined different size lozenges in a subrectangular cartouche, D19mm H24mm. *River Thames foreshore, London.*

183. A circumferential basal plain band with two grooves, a continuous right-hand spiral of circular pits on sides and crown; maker's mark at start of spiral – saltire, D18mm H24mm. *River Thames foreshore, London.*

184. A circumferential basal plain band with two grooves, a continuous right-hand spiral of circular pits on sides and crown; maker's mark away from start of spiral – four pellets forming a square, D17mm H24.5mm. *River Thames foreshore, London.*

185. A circumferential basal plain band with two grooves, a continuous right-hand spiral of circular pits on sides and crown; maker's mark away from start of spiral – two pellets in a possibly horizontal B-shaped cartouche, D19mm 26mm. *River Thames foreshore, London.*

Domed thimbles *c*.1520 – *c*.1650

All are probably from Nuremberg. Hammered copper-alloy with punched pits, and engraved and/or punched decoration; unless specified otherwise, with plain bands and without makers' marks.

186. Five circumferential basal grooves forming three plain bands and two hatched, a continuous right-hand spiral of circular pits on the sides and crown, D15mm H20mm. *River Thames foreshore, London.*

187. Four circumferential basal grooves forming two plain bands, one cross-hatched and one has repeating saltires and pellets with cusped edges; a continuous right-hand spiral of circular pits on the sides and crown, D15mm H18mm. *River Thames foreshore, London.*

188 A basal plain band with a band of repeating circular medallions, and a voided cusped band each side, and a continuous right-hand spiral of circular pits on the sides and crown; D16mm H21mm. PAS LON-26A463. *River Thames foreshore, London.*

189. Five circumferential grooves forming five bands – two plain, two cross-hatched, and one with repeating circular medallions alternating with two bands of hearts, one band of which is interrupted with transverse lines; a continuous right-hand spiral of circular pits on the sides and crown; D16mm H20.5mm. *River Thames foreshore, London.*

190. Six circumferential grooves forming four bands – an upper plain with two grooves, basal two plain, one with two grooves, and one with two bands of repeating curlicues; a right-hand spiral of saltire-shaped pits on the sides and a separate right-hand spiral of similar pits on the crown; D15.57mm H18.73mm. PAS LON-DCC852. *River Thames foreshore, London.*

191. Three circumferential wide, deep grooves forming three plain bands and one with repeating palmettes and transverse lines flanked each side with hatching; a continuous right-hand spiral of circular pits on the sides and crown; D13.2mm H19mm. UKDFD 37303. *Kent.*

192. Eight circumferential grooves forming seven bands – four plain, two with repeating lozenges and chevrons, and one with repeating oval medallions; a continuous right-hand spiral of circular pits on the sides and crown, D18.5mm H24.5mm. *River Thames foreshore, London.*

193. Slightly distorted, four circumferential grooves forming five bands – two plain, two hatched, and one with repeating oval medallions; a continuous right-hand spiral of circular pits on the sides and crown, D21mm H26.8mm. *River Thames foreshore, London.*

194. Four circumferential grooves forming five bands – three plain and two with repeating lozenges enclosing pellets; a continuous right-hand spiral of circular pits on the sides and crown; maker's mark at start of spiral – A, D17mm H21mm. PAS IOW-BE64E7. *Isle of Wight.*

195. White-metal coated, four circumferential grooves forming five bands – two plain, two hatched and one with repeating beaded medallions; a continuous right-hand spiral of circular pits on the sides and crown; maker's mark away from start of spiral – bell or flower in a cartouche of the same shape; D17.5mm H24mm. *River Thames foreshore, London.*

196. Two circumferential cusped grooves forming three bands – two plain and one with repeating oval beaded medallions, a continuous right-hand spiral of circular pits on the sides and crown; maker's mark away from start of spiral – 4, D20mm H17.3mm. PAS LON-94D972. *River Thames foreshore, London.*

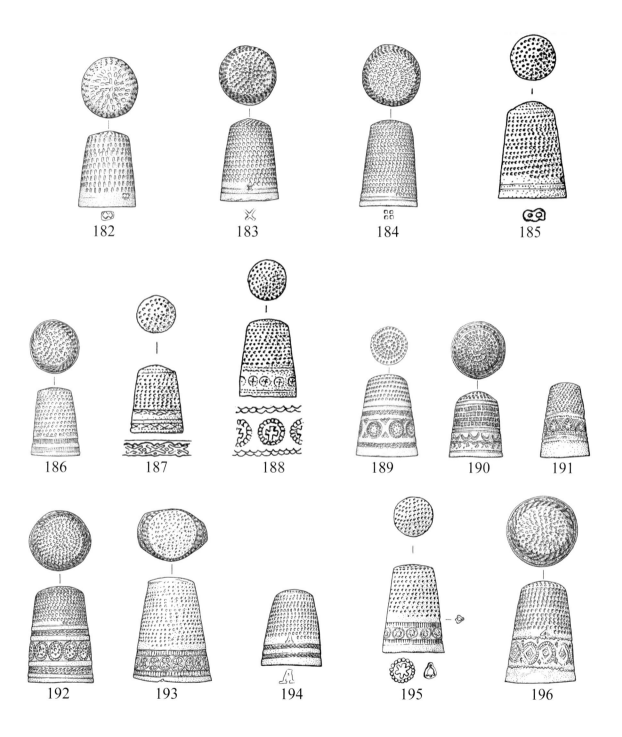

182

183

184

185

186

187

188

189

190

191

192

193

194

195

196

Figure 19. Nuremberg thimble-maker brother Ving [...] drilling pits in a domed thimble c.1414. Note domed and ring-type thimbles on bench. *Mendelschen Institute Housebook 1. Stadtbibliothek Nürnberg Amb. 317.2 , f. 5 v.* Reproduced *courtesy* of the City Library of Nuremberg.

Figure 20. Nuremberg thimble-maker's workshop, after an engraving by Jost Amman (1539-91). First published 1564 and reproduced 1568 by Hans Sachsen in *Eigentliche Beschreibung aller Stände auffErden.* Note iron swaging block, and domed thimbles; some of which appear to have basal rims, which suggests these may have been cast.

Figure 21. Nuremberg thimble-maker brother Veit Schuster 7 January 1592 performing an indeterminate task with a hammer and punch. *Mendelschen Institute Housebook II. Stadtbibliothek Nürnberg, Amb. 317b.2 , f. 52 r.* Reproduced courtesy of the City Library of Nuremberg.

Figure 22. Nuremberg thimble-maker brother Wolf Laim 6 July 1621. *Landauer Foundation Memorial Book I. Stadtbibliothek Nürnberg, Amb. 279.2 , f. 89.* Reproduced courtesy of the City Library of Nuremberg.

Figure 23. Nuremberg thimble-maker brother Martin Winderlein 18 May 1627, punching pits in a domed thimble. Note two different colours of domed thimbles, which suggests both silver and copper-alloy forms. *Mendelschen Institute Housebook II. Stadtbibliothek Nürnberg, Amb. 317b.2 „f. 100 v.* Reproduced courtesy of the City Library of Nuremberg.

Figure 24. Nuremberg thimble-journeyman brother Nicolaus Zeittenberger 24 December 1667, punching pits in a domed thimble. Note two different colours of domed thimbles, which suggests both silver and copper-alloy forms. *Mendelschen Institute Housebook II. Stadtbibliothek Nürnberg, Amb. 317b.2 , f. 144 v.* Reproduced courtesy of the City Library of Nuremberg.

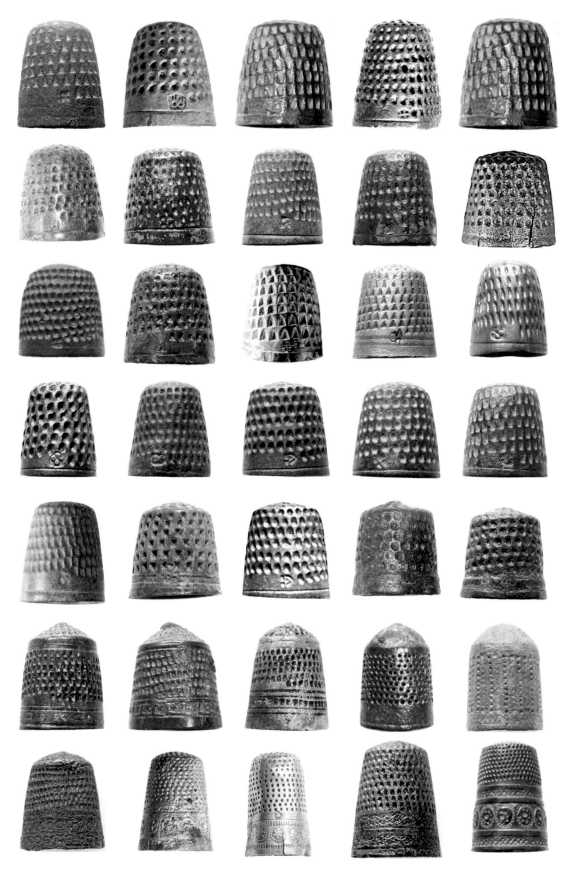

Figure 25a. Nuremberg domed copper-alloy thimbles c.16th century.

Figure 25b. Nuremberg domed copper-alloy thimbles c.16th century.

Figure 26a. Domed copper-alloy and silver thimbles c.16th century.

Figure 26b. Domed copper-alloy and silver thimbles c.16th century (* one is perhaps 17th century).

Domed thimbles c. mid-17th – c. early 18th century

Primary archival data confirming silver or copper-alloy typically tall composite domed thimbles were products of English thimble-makers appears absent (Nos 197-239): Holmes 1985 *et al* ascribe them as mid to late 17th century English though provide no prima facia evidence. The present writer suggests some, particularly certain Charles I commemorative types (see below, Nos 197-201), could be as early as 1625. Inscriptions in English and/or stamped makers' marks on many, supports England as their place of conception. These domed thimbles are usually compositely constructed from two or more pieces of sheeting soldered together and are considered by some to be ungainly and ugly, but for the present writer they have a naïve charm and represent some of the best work by probable English thimble-makers. Curiously, composite copper-alloy examples are scarce in the known record: herein one came from the River Thames foreshore, London (No. 234) (albeit, this is perhaps a ring-type thimble, see below) while two are from inland depositions (Nos 209, 226). A damaged cast copper-alloy specimen (No. 209) is perhaps a rarity as other cast examples are absent from the known record. Whether this paucity of English mid- to late 17th-century copper-alloy domed thimbles means they were not in general use is unclear – if they were, it is reasonable to believe that detectorists would find them.

Characteristically such domed thimbles lack basal rims, however, here two silver examples feature simple lateral rims (Nos 207, 225); the former of which, by being conical, is very unusual. Another probable English silver example is noteworthy by having an internal sleeve, therefore is composite three-piece (No. 221). Longitudinal seams are usually soldered butt, while horizontal seams may be soldered scarfed or butt. Circumferential fairly broad plain bands are typical, commonly basal but occasionally upper, too, sometimes engraved with one or more grooves and religious or secular mottoes (Nos 222-234). Geometric or organic patterns of engraved strapwork – frequently with an engraved linear outline – is normal, the resulting side interstices filled with rows of individually punched annulets or circular, square/rectangular or triangular pits (Nos 202-209, 212-215, 217-219, 221-234). There is a view that the uniformity of annulet pits means they were always mechanically knurled, an assumption refuted by a master goldsmith. Scrutiny of numerous thimbles of this period with annulet pits indicates the use of both block dies and individual punches. Also used, in lieu of pits, is engraved patterns resembling brick bonding or basket weave (Nos 208-209, 217, 225, 232, 234). The quality of brick bonding or basket weave engraving varies from uniform fineness to irregular crude.

Embossed geometric strapwork, and/or organic decoration, is seemingly rare on the sides of these domed thimbles and this study revealed only seven (Nos 197-201, 221, 227). Crowns may be totally pitted or pitted up to a tonsure, while engraved, embossed or punched decorative designs are also common (Nos 202, 215-217, 220-221, 223, 225-226, 232); one here has a totally bare crown (No. 231). Block die-punching on flat sheets of metal forming sides and crowns occurred before shaping into cylinders and domes and soldering the two parts together. Towards the end of the 17th century engraved patterns of pits and individually punched triangular or square/rectangular pits appear to have been phased out though annulets or circular pits continued into the mid-18th.

Commemorative composite sheet silver domed thimbles are also known, of which the earliest recorded in this present study is two damaged examples of Charles I. One has two embossed medallions, each with a rose surmounted by a crown flanked by the initials C and R; possibly made in 1624 (No. 197). The second, also embossed, has two medallions, each with a rose surmounted by crown flanked each side by a cinquefoil on a stem, and between the medallions a profile bust of Charles I (No. 198). The known record also has a few Charles I composite sheet domed thimbles like Nos 199-200. Similar composite sheet silver domed thimbles perhaps commemorated the marriage of Charles II and Catherine of Braganza in 1662 (No. 201) though likewise are scarce finds. In the known record is an exceedingly rare or perhaps unique Charles II commemorative composite sheet silver domed thimble that depicts the Boscobel oak tree (aka Royal Oak) in which the king and Colonel Careless hid after escaping the 1651 battle of Worcester. This historic artefact is in a private collection therefore unavailable to the present writer. Pit shapes on recorded commemorative domed thimbles are annulets or square/rectangular, either block die-punched or individually punched.

Any of the aforesaid mid-17th-century composite sheet silver domed thimble may display a maker's mark, punched on the inside or outside (Nos 200, 210-215, 217, 219, 222, 227, 229), while the owner's engraved initials are noted on some (Nos 197, 200, 210-211, 213, 218, 224). Regrettably, in 1666 London's Great Fire destroyed the Worshipful Company of Goldsmiths' touch plate and other records, therefore identifying makers' marks preceding this date is impossible. A feature noted on three here is a small circular hole near the base, possibly used for attaching via a chain to a chatelaine or finger-ring (Nos 197-198, 202).

Another style of sheet silver composite two-piece domed thimble of this period is fairly ubiquitous, being slimly tapered, with longitudinal butt and horizontal scarfed soldered seams. Circular or square pits, which may be block die-punched or individually punched, spiral right-hand over most of the sides and sometimes continue completely over the crown or up to a tonsure; though crowns may have similar pits but in concentric circles; on one here the crown is totally bare (No. 238). Circumferential basal or both basal and upper plain bands with one or more engraved grooves are frequently noted features (Nos 236-238). These domed thimbles also may feature a small circular hole near the base though none is catalogued here.

Circa 1650, possibly in England, new forms of sheet silver (or gold) composite two- or three-piece domed thimbles evolved, ranging from tall to extremely tiny, the latter perhaps toys (No. 242), which continued until c.1750. McConnel 1991 pp 25 describes two such silver thimbles as 'European' but frustratingly does not provide supporting evidence. Initially, these thimbles were individually punched with pits, either circular or annulets, later replaced with block die-punched annulets. Circumferential basal plain bands, frequently with engraved grooves and hatched ridges, are common (Nos 239-242, 244-247). Although many are rimless, basal lateral rims are noted, either integral or separately soldered (Nos 243-250). Embossed and/or engraved decoration, e.g. a cartouche with the owner's initials or monogram flanked each side with a supporter, frequently birds or other animals, is typical (Nos 249-250) and one has a possible simple motto though this could be a maker's mark (No. 244). A maker's mark may be stamped above or to one side of the cartouche but again there is no record of marks before 1666. A small circular hole near the base is not unusual (No. 249). An apparently rare detecting find is a gold domed thimble of this type, though undecorated, here tentatively ascribed to the last half of the 17th century though later is a possibility (No. 243).

In France, following the 1685 Edict of Fontainebleau, thousands of Huguenots (protestants) fled the country and settled elsewhere in Europe, refugees from religious persecution. Many, some of whom were

Figure 27. English domed composite silver and copper-alloy thimbles (some incomplete) *c.* mid- to *c.* late 17th century.

silversmiths, came to England. As they did in France, these skilled artisans may have produced silver or gold composite two- or three-piece domed thimbles, but now in the aforesaid English style, which today silver examples are relatively ubiquitous in British depositions. The aforesaid gold example (No. 243) is possibly Huguenot-made in England. Interestingly, Isbister 2014 suggests that punched marks found on many of these domed thimbles may be attributed to either Huguenot silversmiths or members of the English Goldsmiths' Company who submitted Huguenot silversmiths' products for assay; therefore marks ought to be called 'sponsors' marks'.

Figure 28. Probable English domed composite silver and gold thimbles *c.* mid-17th to *c.* mid 18th century.

Domed commemorative thimbles *c.* 1625 – c.1685

All are probably English. Composite two-piece sheet silver with longitudinal and horizontal soldered seams, with circumferential basal plain bands and engraved grooves, with punched, engraved and embossed decoration, punched square pits; unless specified otherwise, without owners engraved initials. Crownless examples are perhaps ring-type thimbles.

197. Squashed; a circumferential basal plain band with two grooves inscribed with the owner's initials #I *S* and a small circular hole; three equidistant oval cartouches with cabled borders, each bearing a five-petalled rose surmounted by a crown flanked C one side and R the other – representing Charles I; concentric circles of punched square pits on the sides and crown, D25.7mm H22.8mm. PAS YORYM-B3C2D2, 2014 T538. *South East Dorset.*

198. Crown possibly missing, squashed and a sprung longitudinal seam; a circumferential basal plain band with two grooves and a circular hole; two equidistant oval cartouches, each bearing a five-petalled rose surmounted by a crown and flanked each side with a small five-petalled flower; between the cartouches, a profile bust of Charles I facing left; concentric circles of punched square pits, D *c.*15mm H22mm. *South-West Dorset.*

199. A circumferential basal plain band with four grooves forming two hatched bands; two equidistant oval cartouches, one bearing a profile bust of Charles I facing left, with C one side and R the other; the second cartouche bears a profile bust of Henrietta Maria facing right; (thimble drawn from photographs showing two different angles); *c.*1625; dimensions unknown. *Gloucestershire.*

200. A circumferential basal plain band with four grooves forming two hatched bands and a maker's mark – G in a shield-shaped cartouche, and the owners initials – AK; two equidistant oval cartouches, one bearing a profile bust of Charles II facing left, with C over 2 one side and R the other (the 2 is almost worn away); the second cartouche bears a profile bust of Katherine of Braganza facing left; *c.*1662; dimensions and findspot unknown.

201. A circumferential basal plain band with four grooves forming two hatched bands; an oval cartouche bearing a profile bust of Charles II facing left, with C over 2 one side and R the other. (thimble drawn from a photograph, the other cartouche bearing a bust of Katherine of Braganza unavailable); *c.*1662; dimensions unknown. *Gloucestershire.*

Domed thimbles *c.* mid- *c.* late 17th century

All are probably English. Unless specified otherwise, composite two-piece sheet silver with longitudinal and horizontal soldered seams, punched pits or engraved rectangles or brick-bonding in lieu of pits, geometric strapwork decoration outlined with engraving, circumferential upper and/or basal plain bands with engraved grooves, without owners' engraved initial/s and punched makers' marks. Crownless examples are perhaps ring-type thimbles.

202. Butt seams, circumferential upper and basal plain bands, the basal with two grooves and a small circular hole; three equidistant geometric longitudinal strapwork bands, each with three annulets, on the sides; irregular concentric circles of square pits on the sides; the crown has five concentric circles of square pits around a cinquefoil outlined by a field of random dots; D17mm H25.8mm. PAS DOR-066737, 2012 T685. *Dorset.*

203. Butt seam, crown possibly lost and a section of basal side broken off; circumferential upper and basal plain bands, upper with two grooves and basal three; geometric rectilinear and curvilinear strapwork on the sides, brick-bonding on the sides, D17mm H27mm. PAS LIN-3ED029, 2004 T61. *Lincolnshire.*

204. Butt seams, circumferential upper and basal plain bands, the upper with two grooves and nine equidistant subcircular crosshatched motifs, basal three grooves; geometric curvilinear, rectilinear and organic strapwork on the sides, square pits on the sides; four concentric circles of square pits on the crown up to a tonsure; D19mm H28mm. PAS NARC-A80562, 2011 T473. *Northamptonshire.*

205. Butt seams, circumferential upper and basal plain bands, the upper with two grooves and basal three; three equidistant bands of geometric linear strapwork on the sides, concentric circles of square pits on the sides; a right-hand spiral of square pits on the crown up to tonsure with a circle, D16.1mm H28.2mm. PAS BH-F2C735, 2011 T399. *Hertfordshire.*

206. Sprung butt seam, crown possibly lost; squashed; circumferential upper and basal plain bands, the upper with one groove and basal two; geometric curvilinear bands of strapwork on the sides, square pits on the sides; D *c.*20mm H20.21mm. PAS SUR-B665D3, 2012 T821. *Kent.*

207. Subconical sides, partially sprung butt seams, a circumferential basal plain band with one upper groove and a series of voided oblique grooves; a lateral rim (perhaps separately soldered, which means possible three-piece construction); geometric linear triple grooved cross-hatched strapwork on the sides, lines of circular pits on the sides; a tonsured crown with a circle, D *c.*20mm H20.21mm. PAS SUSS-5872D6, 2011 T437. *East Sussex.*

208. Composite two-piece sheet copper-alloy, distorted, section of side broken off and a small hole in the crown; circumferential basal plain band with two grooves, and a circumferential median plain band with two grooves; in lieu of pits the sides have concentric circles of squares and the crown, lozenges; two bands of geometric crude voided linear strapwork on the sides which overlap the median and basal plain bands; D *c.*20mm H28.5mm. *Hampshire.*

209. Cast copper-alloy; section of crown broken off, slightly distorted and a split side; circumferential upper and basal plain bands, the basal with one groove; the sides have concentric circles of crude rectangles and the crown, lozenges; geometric voided linear strapwork on the sides which overlap the rectangles, D18mm H25mm. *South Lincolnshire.*

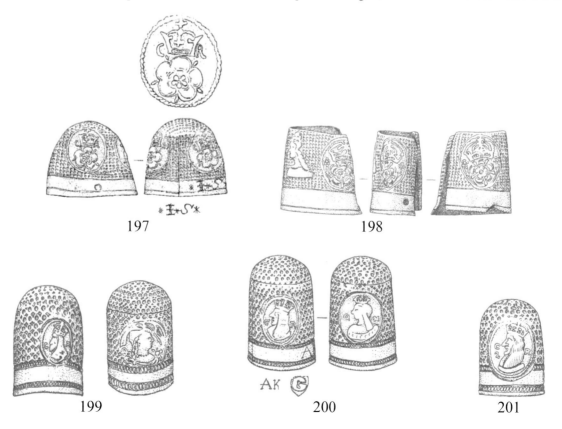

197   198

199   200   201

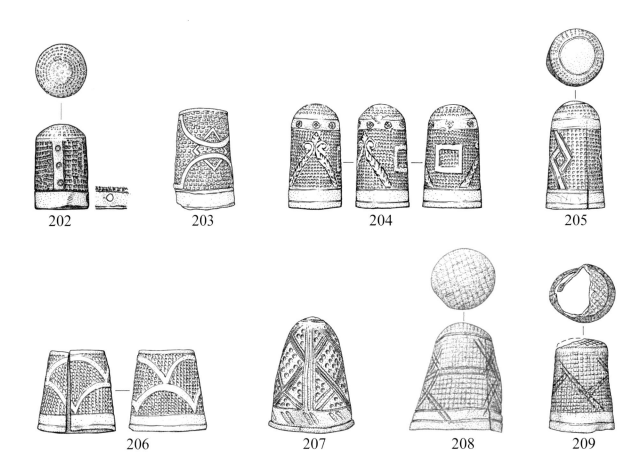

202   203   204   205

206   207   208   209

Domed thimbles *c.* mid – *c.* late 17th century

All are probably English. Sheet silver with longitudinal and horizontal soldered seams; unless specified otherwise, composite two-piece; circumferential upper and/or basal plain bands with engraved grooves, engraved geometric strapwork or organic motifs outlined with engraving, or other engraved, embossed or punched decoration; punched pits or engraved brick-bonding in lieu of pits, punched makers' marks and/or owners engraved initials. Some crownless examples are perhaps ring-type thimbles.

210. No crown and a smooth upper rim suggests this is possibly a ring-type thimble; squashed, sprung longitudinal butt seam; undecorated, circumferential basal plain band with the owner's initials EI; concentric circles of circular pits; maker's mark inside – SC with a pellet above and a five-pointed star below in an asymmetrical cartouche; D *c.*20mm H18mm. *South West Wiltshire.*

211. Crown lost, slightly distorted, ragged upper edge, sprung longitudinal butt seam; a circumferential basal plain band with two serrated double-edged grooves; alternate concentric circles of small and large circular pits; undecorated except for a basal rectangular plain panel delineated with similar serrated grooves, single on the left side, double on the right and top, enclosing the owner's initials EP and a maker's mark – MB in a heart-shaped cartouche; D *c.*16mm H16mm. *Wales.*

212. No crown and a smooth upper rim suggests this is possibly a ring-type thimble, slightly distorted, sprung butt seam; circumferential upper and basal plain bands, the upper with one groove and basal two; three repeating organic quatrefoils on the sides; concentric circles of square pits; maker's mark inside – five-pointed star surmounted by TA in a shield-shaped cartouche, D15mm H21mm. PAS NMS-IA5IC8, 2011 T598. *South Norfolk.*

213. No crown and a smooth upper rim suggests this is possibly a ring-type thimble, sprung longitudinal butt seam; circumferential upper and basal plain bands, the upper has one groove and basal two with the owner's inverted initials BK; geometric linear strapwork; concentric circles of square pits; maker's mark inside – five-pointed star surmounted by TA in a shield-shaped cartouche (the same as No. 212), D14mm H18mm. *Western Gloucestershire.*

214. Crown possibly lost, slightly distorted, sprung longitudinal butt seam; circumferential basal plain band with two grooves; geometric linear strapwork, concentric circles of square pits; maker's mark inside – inverted RL in a square cartouche; D16mm H21.65mm. PAS HAMP-CD9BB6, 2009 T526. *East Hampshire.*

215. Longitudinal butt seam and scarfed horizontal, circumferential upper and basal plain bands, the upper with one groove and basal two; geometric curvilinear strapwork, concentric circles of square pits on the sides; and the crown has four concentric circles of square pits up to a tonsure with an off-centre embossed fleur-de-lis; maker's mark inside – RV or RW in a subrectangular cartouche; D16mm H21.65mm. PAS DEV-D013EA, 2015 T758. *South Somerset.*

216. A detached distorted tonsured crown from a composite thimble, four concentric circles of square pits and an embossed fleur-de-lis, D13.5mm. *Derbyshire.*

217. Traces of possible niello; butt longitudinal and slightly sprung horizontal scarfed seams, circumferential upper and basal bands, the upper plain with one groove, the basal has two grooves filled with plain areas alternating with oblique hatching and a maker's mark – (?) B in an asymmetrical cartouche; geometric linear and curvilinear strapwork on the sides, brick-bonding on the sides; the crown has three concentric circles of similar brick-bonding and an elaborate sunburst and possible trees in a circle, D24mm H31.5mm. *North Wiltshire.*

218. No crown and a smooth upper rim suggests this is possibly a ring-type thimble, sprung longitudinal butt seam; circumferential upper and basal plain bands, the upper with one groove and the basal two, and the owner's initials KW; geometric linear strapwork, concentric circles of square pits, D17mm H23mm. PAS NMS-AAFFC2, 2012 T34. *South Norfolk.*

219. Crown lost, slightly ragged rim, sprung longitudinal butt seam; circumferential upper and basal plain bands, upper with one groove, basal two and the owner's initial G; geometric linear strapwork with equidistant annulets, concentric circles of annulet pits, D17mm H20mm. UKDFD 8658. *Hampshire.*

220. A detached distorted crown from a composite thimble; two concentric circles of annulet pits and a double five-petalled rose, D13mm; possibly 16th century. NMS-E89E06, 2007 T268. *Norfolk.*

221. Composite three-piece, longitudinal butt seam and scarfed horizontal, circumferential upper and basal plain bands, basal with one groove and two embossed beaded circumferential bands, geometric embossed linear strapwork on the sides; oblique columns of circular pits on the sides; a tonsured crown with an abraded embossed (?) maker's mark (?) T or H in a circle surrounded by 16 embossed petals intermittent with 16 bands of embossed pellets; an internal sleeve with a longitudinal butt seam, 18mm H27mm. *Derbyshire.*

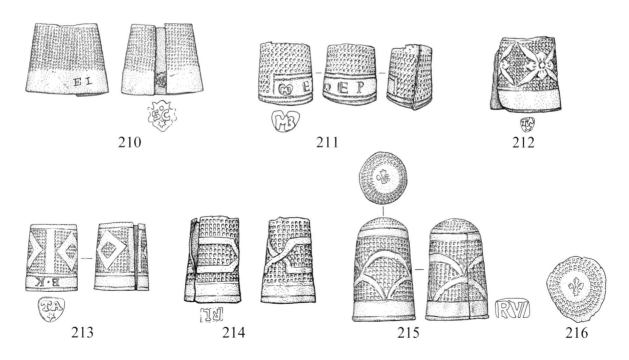

210   211   212

213   214   215   216

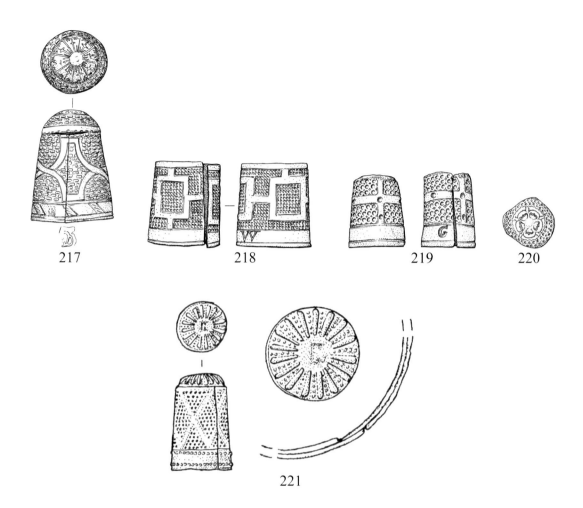

217   218   219   220

221

Domed thimbles *c.* mid – *c.* late 17th century

All are probably English. Unless specified otherwise, composite two-piece sheet silver with longitudinal and horizontal soldered seams; circumferential upper and/or basal plain bands with engraved grooves; punched pits or engraved cross-hatching or brick-bonding in lieu of pits; geometric strapwork or organic motifs outlined with engraving and other punched decoration; with basal engraved inscriptions, owners' initials and makers' punched marks. Those without a crown are perhaps ring-type thimbles.

222. No crown and a smooth upper rim suggests this is possibly a ring-type thimble, sprung butt seam; circumferential upper and basal plain bands, the upper with one groove, the basal two and inscribed **Bee not idle**; concentric circles of square pits; maker's mark inside – R, D15.5mm H14mm. *Gloucestershire.*

223. Copper alloy, longitudinal scarfed and horizontal butt sprung seams; circumferential upper and basal plain bands, the upper with one groove, the basal two and unintelligibly inscribed **A IH [...] E** (E is retrograde); geometric linear and curvilinear strapwork on the sides; rectangles in lieu of pits on the sides; the crown has eight radiating spokes with in each segment, transverse and oblique dashes; D17mm H23mm. PAS LON-228895. *Thames foreshore, London.*

224. Longitudinal butt and horizontal scarfed seams; circumferential basal plain band with two grooves and inscribed **keepe promise**, a six-point star and the owner's initials ET; the sides have geometric linear strapwork with internal equidistant circular pits; columns of square pits; five concentric circles of square pits on the crown up to a tonsure; maker's mark inside – RI, D17.71mm H26.29mm. PAS SF-9F9DA1, 2010 T602. *Suffolk.*

225. Longitudinal butt and horizontal scarfed seams; circumferential upper and basal plain bands, the upper with two grooves and repeating I's; the basal has two grooves and inscribed **I LI VE IN HOPE +;** a lateral rim; geometric linear strapwork with running scrolls resembling fronds on the sides; the crown has similar strapwork, but with voided grooves each side, formed as a triqueta around a cinquefoil in a circle, brick-bonding in lieu of pits on the sides and crown, D15mm H16mm. *East Devon.*

226. Sheet copper alloy, squashed flat, sprung horizontal scarfed seam; a circumferential basal plain band with three grooves and unintelligibly inscribed **+ IOV + VOV**; geometric linear and curvilinear strapwork on the sides; the crown has a cross-hatched circle and two concentric circles of long and short dashes; brick-bonding in lieu of pits on the sides, D25mm H34.89mm. PAS DOR-43A55E. *Dorset.*

227. No crown and a smooth upper rim suggests this is possibly a ring-type thimble; longitudinal butt seam; circumferential upper and basal plain bands, the upper with one groove and the basal three and inscribed **Love Vertue;** two equidistant embossed and engraved thistles; maker's mark inside – R within a subrectangular cartouche; concentric circles of square pits, D14mm H20mm. *South Wales.*

228. No crown and a smooth upper rim suggests this is possibly a ring-type thimble, slightly distorted, sprung longitudinal butt seam; circumferential upper and basal plain bands, the upper with one groove, the basal two and inscribed **WORCKE IS PROFITABLE**; circumferential organic motifs – two four-petalled fleurets alternating with two hearts; concentric circles of square pits, D20mm H22mm, PAS WAW-764970, 2011 T145. *Warwickshire.*

229. Crown possibly lost, squashed flat, sprung longitudinal butt seam; circumferential upper and basal plain bands, the upper with one groove and the basal three and inscribed **Be true mo hearte till death**; maker's mark inside – I in a hexagonal cartouche; geometric linear strapwork, columns of square pits, D26mm H22mm. *South Devon.*

230. Crown possibly lost, distorted, sprung longitudinal butt seam; circumferential upper and basal plain bands, the basal with two grooves and inscribed **MEE --- REMEMBE R**; geometric and curvilinear strapwork with equidistant annulets, concentric circles of square pits, D19.13mm H23.04mm. PAS WMID-5CB6A4, 2011 T190. *Staffordshire.*

231. Copper alloy, longitudinal butt and horizontal scarfed seams; circumferential upper and basal plain bands, the upper with two grooves, the basal three and inscribed **+WORKE A PASE**; geometric linear strapwork on the sides, concentric circles of triangular pits; the crown is bare with no sign of pits or decoration, D16.2mm H28mm. PAS LON-6F9633. *River Thames foreshore, London.*

232. Distorted and a torn side, sprung longitudinal butt seam; circumferential upper and basal bands, the upper with two grooves and geometric key decoration, the basal has two grooves and a beaded band and inscribed **A FENDE + TO + THE END**; geometric curvilinear strapwork on the sides; brick bonding in lieu of pits on the sides and the crown, which also has a five-point star infilled with five petals and a cinquefoil; residue of niello in some of the decorative elements, maker's mark inside – RL; D20mm H27.28mm. PAS SUR-639460, 2014 T253. *Essex.*

233. This is possibly a ring-type thimble though it is perhaps a cut-down domed thimble, longitudinal butt seam; circumferential upper and basal bands, the upper with one groove and peripheral repeating marks interpreted as remnants of a possible inscription, the basal has two grooves, a border of repeating pits and inscribed **THI + FRINDE + I'D + BEE**; geometric strapwork on the sides – four repeating ornate ovals, each with an upper and basal transverse buckle-like object, similar objects are sited where the sides of the strapwork touch; oblique rows of circular pits, D16.22mm H22.93mm. PAS CAM-796FF4, 2011 T588. *Cambridgeshire.*

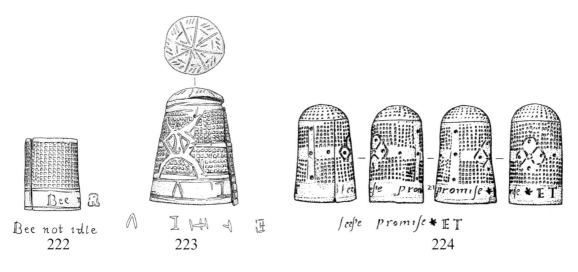

Bee not idle
222

IW
223

ſeſe promiſe✱ET
224

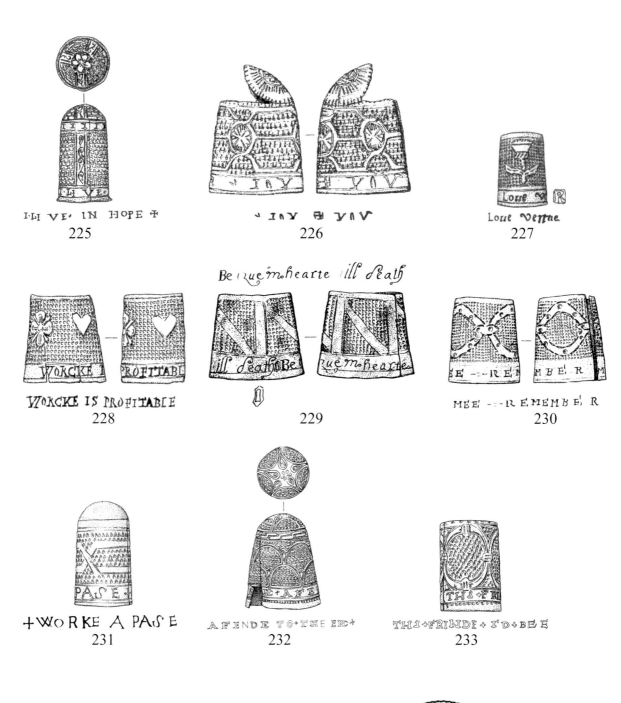

I·LI VE· IN HOPE ✢
225

↙ IηV ⊕ Yη∇
226

Loue Vertue
227

WORCKE IS PROFITABLE
228

Be que m hearte ill death
ill death Be que m hearte
229

MEE ⸺ REMEMBE·R
230

✢WORKE A PAS·E
231

A FENDE TO·THE END✢
232

THI✦FRINDE✦I'D✦BE E
233

234. Copper alloy; longitudinal butt seam, a circumferential narrow upper plain band with one groove and an unusual cusped rim which suggests this is perhaps a ring-type thimble; a basal plain band with two grooves and inscribed **V + MV [X] I [I]**; geometric linear and curvilinear strapwork, engraved hatching in lieu of pits on the sides, D18.5mm H29mm. *River Thames foreshore, London.*

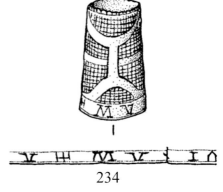

234

Domed thimbles *c.* mid – *c.* late 17th century

All are probably English. Unless specified otherwise, all are composite two-piece sheet silver with longitudinal and horizontal soldered seams, circumferential plain bands with engraved grooves, punched pits or annulets, without makers' marks, and undecorated.

235. Longitudinal butt and horizontal scarfed seams, a circumferential basal plain band with three grooves, a continuous right-hand spiral of circular pits on the sides and crown, D14.3mm H22.8mm. *North Dorset.*

236. Longitudinal scarfed and lapped butt and horizontal scarfed seams, a circumferential basal plain band with two grooves, a continuous right-hand spiral of circular pits on the sides and crown up to a tonsure with a centring pit, D15mm H21.9mm. *South Somerset.*

237. A sprung longitudinal butt seam and horizontal scarfed seam, circumferential upper and basal plain bands, the upper with one groove and the basal two; a right-hand spiral of square pits on the sides and four concentric circles of identical pits on the crown up to a tonsure; D17.4mm H28mm. PAS IOW-B09406. *Isle of Wight.*

238. Copper alloy, longitudinal butt and horizontal scarfed seams, circumferential upper and basal plain bands, the basal with one faint groove and repeating oblique grooves; a right-hand spiral of square pits on the sides, the crown is bare, D17.74mm H28.46mm. *Kent.*

Domed thimbles *c.* mid-17th – *c.* mid-18th century

Unless specified otherwise, all are English and composite two-piece sheet silver with longitudinal butt and horizontal scarfed seams; without rims, makers' punched marks and/or engraved owners' initials and undecorated; with circumferential plain bands and engraved grooves, punched pits or annulets.

239. A circumferential basal plain band with two cabled bands, punched annulet pits in columns on the sides and concentric circles the crown, D16.55mm H23.57mm. BERK-BC5163, 2011T339. *Oxfordshire.*

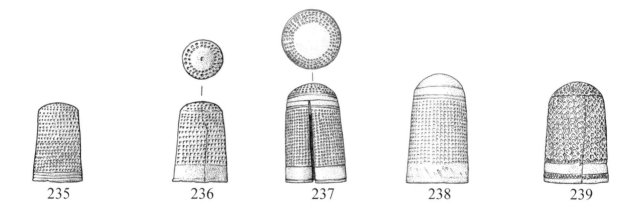

235   236   237   238   239

240. PAS report states cast though these thimbles are normally composite. A circumferential basal plain band with two cabled grooves and a maker's mark – G in a subrectangular cartouche; concentric circles of annulet pits on the sides and bands the crown, D15.3mm H21mm. PAS SUR-AF6834, 2011 T139. *Surrey.*

241. A circumferential basal plain band with two cabled grooves and a maker's mark – S in a rectangular cartouche; concentric circles of annulet pits on the sides and crown, D16mm H20mm. UKDFD 30739. *Northamptonshire.*

242. A circumferential basal plain band with two grooves and a maker's mark – a lozenge with an integral chevron each end and a central annulet; six concentric circles of small circular pits on the upper half of the sides and bands of larger circular pits on the crown, D10mm H12mm. *Bedfordshire.*

243. Possibly French- or English Huguenots-made, sheet gold, three-piece, a separate soldered basal rim, a continuous right-hand spiral of circular pits on the sides and crown; D13mm H14.5mm. *East Devon.*

244. A very deep circumferential basal groove and pronounced rim, a basal subrectangular cartouche inscribed **ENG** (whether the owner's initials or a maker's mark is uncertain), a continuous right-hand spiral of circular pits on the sides and crown, D14mm H17mm. Dev. Mus. Acc. 1988, 230. *Wiltshire.*

245. Three-piece, a separate soldered basal rim, a circumferential basal embossed cabled border; a banner-shaped cartouche with the owner's initials MC (the M is cross-hatched), embossed cherub supporters, S-scrolls and pellets, surmounted by a maker's mark – TB in an oval cartouche, concentric circles of annulet pits on the sides and crown, D14.4mm H15.6mm. *East Devon.*

246. Three-piece, a separate soldered basal rim, three circumferential basal grooves and two ridges, one embossed with cabling; a rectangular cartouche with cusped edges and the owner's initials ESE; concentric circles of annulet pits on the sides and circular pits in rows the crown, D17mm H19mm. *South West Dorset.*

247. Three-piece, slightly distorted and a small section of separate soldered basal rim broken off, a basal embossed cabled band; a rectangular cartouche with embossed cabled edges and the owner's initials E * C, and a partially indistinct transverse maker's mark – C [?] in an oval cartouche; concentric circles of annulet pits on the sides and crown, D18mm H18mm. PAS NMS-653275, 2012 T135. *Norfolk.*

248. Three-piece, a separate soldered rim; a rectangular basal area of the sides is plain and has an indistinct maker's mark in an asymmetrical-cartouche; concentric circles of circular pits on the sides and crown up to a tonsure, D18.2mm H21mm. *Dorset.*

249. A deep circumferential basal groove, an embossed cabled band and a pronounced rim; a rectangular cartouche with embossed bird supporters and the owner's hatched initials EM; an indistinct maker's mark surmounts the cartouche; a basal small circular hole in the side; concentric circles of circular pits on the sides and rows the crown, D15mm H17mm. *South Somerset.*

250. A circumferential basal plain band with an embossed beaded band; circumferential embossed repeating foliate and two hearts with cherub supporters and surmounted with a maker's mark – RI; concentric circles of annulet pits on the sides and rows the crown, D16mm H18mm. *South West Dorset.*

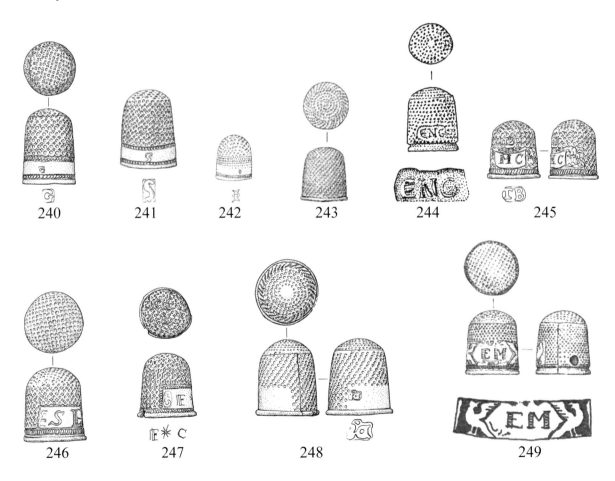

240   241   242   243   244   245

246   247   248   249

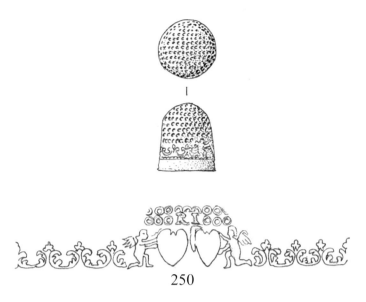

250

Dutch Holmes' Type I domed thimbles *c*.16th – *c*. mid-17th century

According to Holmes 1985, in the period 1620 – 1650 a different and very distinctive style of composite two-piece sheet copper-alloy domed thimble – classified by Holmes 1988 as Type I – was developed and produced in different sizes in the Netherlands. However, such Holmes' Type I thimbles were excavated in Amsterdam from archaeological stratified deposits ranging between *c*.16th – *c*. mid-18th century (Langedijk and Boon 1999, ills 71, 75-77, cat. 137, 151-52). This of course does not mean Holmes' Type I Dutch domed thimbles from the latter context are actually 18th-century products, they were just in use well beyond 1650; however, it does conclusively prove their date range does antecede 1620. Their sides have longitudinal soldered butt-seams and horizontal soldered butt- or scarfed-seams joining crowns to sides. Such seams are usually very evident, particularly the side ones. Characteristically, some of these thimbles feature circumferential basal deeply engraved wide concave plain bands, frequently creating ridges and lateral rims. Another circumferential plain band, usually with one or more engraved grooves and ridges, runs around the sides below the crown. Langedijk and Boon 1999 mention that a circumferential separate soldered brass strip sometimes covered the horizontal seam; this study failed to reveal such a component.

In 1609 Dutchman Gerart van Slangenborch invented the mechanical multiple knurling wheel used to indent circular pits on the sides of both domed and ring-type thimbles (Langedijk and Boon 1999). This device created an easily recognisable diagnostic feature on the sides, while crowns were block die-punched with square pits or concentric circles of individually punched circular pits. After pitting, crowns were formed into domes, a procedure that sometimes tended to distort the peripheral pits. These thimbles usually lack decoration though two herein feature a circumferential band of punched beads between the upper two basal grooves (Nos 254-255). Black coating is occasionally apparent on Holmes' Type I domed thimbles, especially from London's River Thames foreshore depositions (see Fig. 28).

During the first half of the 17th century some Dutch Holmes' Type I domed thimbles were punched with makers' marks, apparently singly – though known from Amsterdam and England they are rarely seen; cf Langedijk and Boon 1999, ills 21-22. This present study revealed only two with definite but unidentifiable makers' marks (Nos 254-255). There is no surviving record of to whom these marks should be attributed.

Figure 29. Dutch Holmes' Type I domed copper-alloy thimbles *c.*16th – *c.* mid-17th century.

Domed thimbles Holmes' Type I *c.*16th – *c.* mid-17th century

From the Netherlands. All are composite two-piece sheet copper-alloy with longitudinal and horizontal soldered scarfed seams, circumferential plain bands and engraved grooves and ridges, mechanically knurled circular pits; and unless specified otherwise, without punched makers' marks or decoration.

251. Circumferential upper and basal plain bands, basal with two wide grooves and two ridges, the lower of which forms a rim, D17mm H23mm. *South Somerset.*

252. Circumferential upper and basal plain bands, upper with two grooves and two ridges, basal with two wide grooves and two ridges, the lower of which forms a pronounced rim, D17.5mm H25.5mm. *South West Wiltshire.*

253. Circumferential upper and basal plain bands, upper with three grooves and three ridges, basal with one wide and one narrow groove and two ridges, the lower of which forms a pronounced rim, D18.8mm H27mm. *South West Wiltshire.*

254. Circumferential upper and basal plain bands, upper with two grooves, basal with one wide and one narrow groove and two ridges, and a band of embossed beading, maker's mark in basal band – a fleur over a trefoil and a small subtriangular motif, D21.8mm H28.2mm. *Lincolnshire.*

255. Circumferential upper and basal plain bands, basal with three engraved grooves and two ridges, the lower groove forms a rim, maker's mark in basal band – a five-petalled rose, D16.5mm H24.1mm. PAS SWYOR-EEEF03. *South Yorkshire.*

256. Although a basal plain band is absent, this thimble is characteristic with a Holmes Type I Dutch domed thimble which has lost its crown; nonetheless it is perhaps a true ring-type thimble with a sprung longitudinal seam, D18mm H14mm. *North Dorset.*

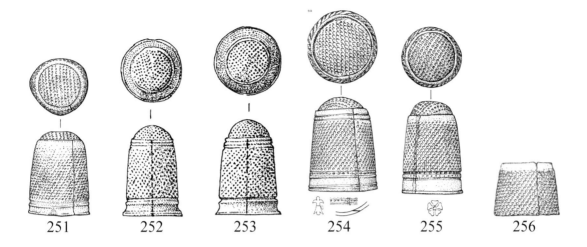

251 252 253 254 255 256

Dutch and English Holmes' Type II domed seamless thimbles *c.*1620 – *c.* mid-18th century

In 1686 enterprising Dutch merchant and fire-engine maker John Loftinck (aka Loftingh), born *c.*1659, migrated to England and changed his name to Lofting. He invented the 'Sucking Worm Fire Engine' that utilised atmospheric pressure to lift water through wire-reinforced leather hose without the walls collapsing: this hose is known as 'hard suction hose', and the principal remains in use by fire brigades and industry globally. Circa 1693 Lofting started a thimble manufactory at Islington, Middlesex (now an inner London suburb): a street there is named Lofting Road, which is the former location of the partially horse-powered works. Lofting moved thimble production *c.*1700 to a watermill by the River Thames at Great Marlow, Buckinghamshire. For producing his thimbles in England, Lofting patented (patent 319) a new casting technique and a knurling machine for impressing pits, but he was not the inventor of either (see above); both of these innovations he brought from the Netherlands. Lofting died 15 June 1742; however, his watermill may have been still producing thimbles in 1748, when it closed is uncertain.

From *c.*1650 to *c.*1730 the Dutch manufactured cast copper-alloy domed thimbles and according to Holmes 1988 Lofting cast identical domed thimbles from *c.*1690 to *c.*1730 using patterns he supposedly brought from the Netherlands. It is impossible to differentiate these Dutch- or English-made domed thimbles classified by Holmes as Type II. Holmes' start date of *c.*1690 for Lofting's Type II thimble does not square with the date Lofting opened his Islington factory, i.e. *c.*1693, it is probable that *c.*1690 is incorrect. Confusingly, Holmes' Type II Dutch and English (Lofting) cast domed thimbles are similar in appearance to Holmes' Type I Dutch composite domed thimbles, telling which is which is simple – Type I feature soldered seams and Type II is seamless.

On Type II, circumferential upper and basal plain bands with engraved groove/s and ridges are typical features, though the upper groove/s are frequently absent. Crowns are generally domed but shallow-pointed are known, too (No. 268). All have mechanically knurled circular pits on the sides, identical to those on Holmes' Type I, and crowns have block die-punched square or circular pits, the latter configured in left-hand spirals or concentric circles. Concentric circles usually have pits all the same size, however, circles of large pits alternating with circles of small pits are also known. Here, two have tonsured crowns (Nos 267-268), which, if Holmes is correct (see above), suggest Type II may antecede c.1650 or tonsured crowns possibly prevailed after this date. Overall black coating is noted on one Holmes' Type II domed thimble catalogued herein (No. 266) and white metal is apparent on another (No. 261). Various sizes were produced; some so small, presumably meant for use by children.

Like Holmes' Type I, during the first half of the 17th century makers' marks, sometimes two, were punched on some Dutch Holmes' Type II thimbles, but again are rarely seen; cf ills 22-23, Langedijk and Boon 1999. Only one with a maker's mark was noted during this present study (No. 271).

In 1668 the Portuguese galleon *Sacramento* sank off Brazil and hundreds of domed thimbles that formed part of her cargo were subsequently recovered in 1976 by marine archaeologists. Holmes dating suggests these thimbles are likely to be Dutch Holmes' Type II though the scant detail and poor illustrations in the archaeological report (de Mello U. P. 1979) means it is of no use in confirming precisely to which type these thimbles belong or whether any have a maker's mark. As mentioned above, domed examples of Dutch Holmes' Type II thimbles were recovered from the 1711 wreck of the Dutch East Indiaman *De Liefde* (Fig. 30). The archaeological report (Price R and Mackelroy K 1977) also provides little useful information about these thimbles though the illustrations are far better. Fortunately, the present writer was able to confirm the typology by utilising the physical evidence kindly provided by Jenny Murray, Shetland Museum and Archive.

Holmes' Type II domed seamless thimbles c. 1620 – c. mid-18th century

From the Netherlands and England. All are cast copper-alloy with circumferential plain bands and engraved grooves and ridges; with mechanically knurled circular pits on the sides and die-stamped circular on the crown; and unless specified otherwise, without makers' marks or decoration.

257. Slightly ragged basal edge; circumferential upper and basal plain bands, both with two grooves, D18mm H16.2mm. *South Somerset.*

258. Circumferential upper and basal plain bands, basal with two deep grooves, a ridge and a shallow rim, D14mm H16.8mm. *River Thames foreshore, London.*

259. Circumferential upper and basal plain bands, upper recessed and basal with two deep engraved grooves, a ridge and a rim; D14mm H18mm. *South West Wiltshire.*

260. Circumferential upper and basal plain bands, basal with four grooves and two ridges, D18mm H26mm. *River Thames foreshore, London.*

261. White-metal coated; circumferential upper and basal plain bands, basal with three grooves, two ridges and a rim; D17mm H23mm. *River Thames foreshore, London.*

262. Circumferential upper and basal plain bands, basal with two grooves, a ridge and a shallow rim, D18mm H26mm. *South West Wiltshire.*

263. Circumferential upper and basal plain bands, upper with one groove and basal four grooves, two ridges and a rim, D18mm H25mm. *South West Wiltshire.*

264. Circumferential upper and basal plain bands, upper recessed and basal with three grooves, a ridge and a rim, D17mm H25mm. *South West Wiltshire.*

265. Circumferential upper and basal plain bands, upper recessed and basal with two grooves, a ridge and a rim, D18mm H26mm. *South Somerset.*

266. Circumferential upper and basal plain bands, upper with two grooves, basal three grooves, a ridge and a rim; black coating, D18.8mm H29mm. *River Thames foreshore, London.*

267. Tonsured crown, circumferential upper and basal plain bands, upper with two grooves, basal four grooves, three ridges and a rim, D16mm H24mm. *River Thames foreshore, London.*

268. Pointed crown with eight concentric circles of pits up to a small tonsure, circumferential upper and basal plain bands, basal with three grooves and a ridge, D18mm H24mm. *River Thames foreshore, London.*

269. Circumferential upper and basal plain bands, upper with two circumferential bands of very faint tiny punched pits, basal three grooves and a band of embossed slightly oblique ovals, D15mm H21mm. *River Thames foreshore, London.*

270. Circumferential upper and basal plain bands, basal with four grooves, a band of embossed slightly oblique ovals and a shallow rim, D19.2mm H24.9mm. *River Thames foreshore, London.*

271. Circumferential upper and basal plain bands, upper with two grooves, basal with one wide and one narrow groove and two ridges, the lower forming a rim; makers mark in the basal band – S, D18mm H28mm. *River Thames foreshore, London.*

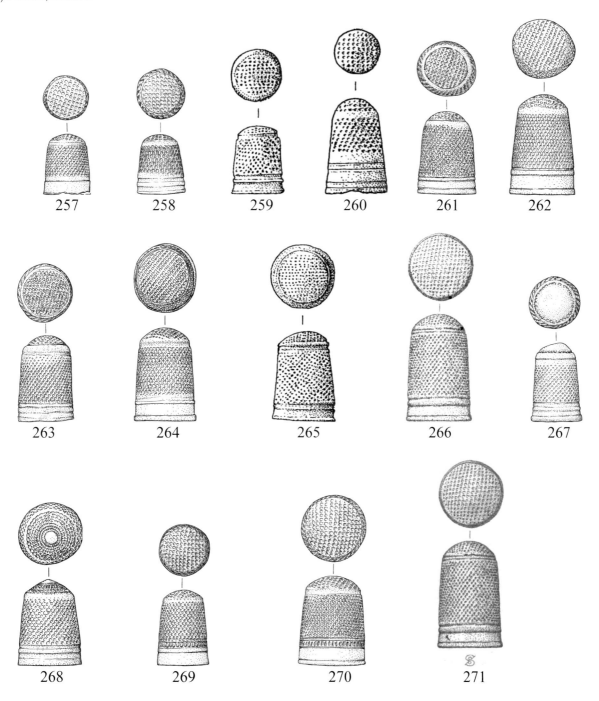

257   258   259   260   261   262

263   264   265   266   267

268   269   270   271

Figure 30. Engraving of thimble-maker John Lofting by J Kip in the *London Prospects Portfolio c.*1690.

Figure 31. Dutch Holmes' Type II domed copper-alloy thimble 18th century, from the Dutch East Indiaman *De Liefde* (*The Love*). Note mechanically knurled circular pits, basal bands and deep grooves. Photo copyright © Lewis Murray and reproduced courtesy of Shetland Museum and Archive.

Figure 32. Dutch or English Holmes' Type II domed copper-alloy thimbles *c.* mid-17th – *c.* mid-18th century.

Dutch and English Holmes' Type III domed thimbles *c*.1730 – *c*.1800

The Holmes' Type III cast copper-alloy domed thimble, which originated in the Netherlands, is perhaps the most ubiquitous kind of domed thimble found in Britain by detectorists. John Lofting possibly introduced Type III into England where they were produced between *c*.1730 – *c*.1800 (Holmes 1988). If Holmes is correct, it implies that Lofting's Great Marlow manufactory continued to operate well after 1748 (see above). Generally, these thimbles are quite squat and known in various sizes, and it is likely that Lofting, using the Type III pattern, was the first to mass produce for children (Nos 273-274, 276) (Holmes 1985). Some of the latter are extremely tiny, perhaps being toys and not functional. Basal lateral rims are common (No. 276) though many are rimless and some have circumferential upper and/ or basal plain bands (Nos 272-275); the latter frequently engraved with a groove. Mechanically knurled circular pits, as found on Holmes' Types I and II, may extend over the whole or most of the sides. Crown pits are block die-punched lozenge-shaped. Differentiating Holmes' Type III domed thimbles made by Lofting from their Dutch counterparts, and those from other English manufactories, is impossible. Sufficient variations exist, suggesting different moulds or different makers.

Domed thimbles, Holmes' Type III *c*. 1730 – *c*. 1800

From the Netherlands or England, all are cast copper-alloy with mechanically knurled circular pits on the sides and die-stamped lozenge-shaped on the crown. Unless specified otherwise, without rims.

272. Circumferential basal plain band, D17mm H18mm. *South Somerset.*

273. Circumferential basal plain band with one groove, D11.2mm H12mm. *South Devon.*

274. Circumferential basal plain band with one groove, D11.2mm H12mm. *South Somerset.*

275. Circumferential upper and basal plain bands, basal with one groove, D13mm H20mm. *South Devon.*

276. Circumferential basal rim, D11.2mm H12mm. *South Devon.*

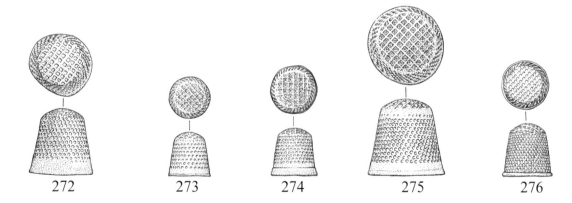

272   273   274   275   276

Miscellaneous domed thimbles *c*. mid-18th – *c*. mid-19th century

Around the mid-18th century there appeared cast copper-alloy or pewter and deep-drawn silver domed thimbles similarly-shaped to certain late 17th-century and Holmes' Type III domed thimbles. As explained earlier, pewter examples as detecting finds are rare in the known record (Nos 279-280). Like Holmes' Type III the smallest pewter one here is perhaps a toy (No. 279). Due to its tiny size and pointed crown, another here of copper-alloy is also possibly a toy (No. 278).

Larger versions of these cast copper-alloy, or deep-drawn silver domed thimbles, and some oddities, noted during this study, are included here. Some have circumferential basal and/or upper plain bands with or without engraved grooves (Nos 277-278, 284, 285-288) and are rimless, though a lateral rim is not uncommon (Nos 278-280, 282-283, 286-287, 290). Some have mechanically knurled pits on sides and crowns while sides of others are mechanically knurled and crowns individually punched. Elaborate engraved organic or pictorial decoration on the sides is a pleasing feature on several (Nos 285-288), as is multiple circumferential grooves (Nos 281-282). Gilding survives on the sides of one (No. 289), which retains a steel cap in a remarkable condition for an excavated thimble. Whether a copper-alloy unusual composite two-piece flat-crowned specimen is a hybrid Holmes' Type III is unclear; its pits are mechanically knurled circular on the sides and die-punched lozenge-shaped on the crown, the latter bordered with punched smaller circular pits (No. 283). The flat crown could be a replacement for a damaged integral domed crown (cf a 19th-century silver thimble with a definite replacement flat crown Fig. 2). It is uncertain whether an unusual stubby, silver domed hexagonal carinated thimble is cast or hammered sheet (No. 284). Each side panel is covered with slightly irregular individually punched square pits. The embossed floral decoration on the crown is either individually punched or block die-punched. Square pits suggest a possible c.17th-century attribution, however, the crown decoration is more typical of the late 18th century or even early 19th. As no dated parallel is in the known record, here it is tentatively ascribed as either late 18th or early 19th century. Where any of the above thimbles originated is uncertain; all are possibly English.

Hammered sheet silver or copper-alloy domed thimbles thought to be English, ascribed as between c.1750 and the mid-19th century, are plenteous. Generally these are fairly tall, with shallow rounded or flat crowns (Nos 292-294). Pits may be mechanically knurled on the sides though punched circular pits configured in a right-hand spiral on the sides and concentric circles the crown feature on one here (No. 292). Pits frequently cover only the upper two-thirds or half of the sides, below which is a circumferential broad plain band frequently decorated with punchwork or engraving, e.g. several grooves, geometric or organic patterns and the owner's initials (Nos 292-299). Silver examples with steel-capped crowns, which on those excavated, is usually represented by rust or rust staining, are ubiquitous (Nos 295-299). Children evidently used small examples practically or as toys (Nos 296, 298). A more unusual domed thimble of this type is composite three-piece sheet silver and formerly fitted with a steel cap (No. 295) (see below).

Sometime in the last quarter of the 18th century mechanical deep drawing – the same as hand hammering but using a machine instead – commenced for mass thimble production and differentiating the two methods is difficult. Although beyond this present study's remit, 19th-century deep-drawn gold slim domed thimbles are not common detecting discoveries though occasionally do surface.

In Birmingham, brass-founding began around the start of the 18th century and this probably included thimbles, and coupled with a rebirth of cast copper-alloy thimble production in South Westphalia, Germany, these two sources are thought to have provided a proportion of Britain's needs. But what these German thimbles look like is unclear: the wealth of thimbles found by detectorists frustratingly does not help to determine they actually did circulate in Britain.

Domed thimbles c. mid-18th – c. mid-19th century

Unless specified otherwise, all are uncertain provenance; cast copper-alloy, mechanically knurled circular pits on the sides and die-punched lozenge-shaped on the crown; some have circumferential engraved grooves creating bands of either plain or engraved or embossed decoration, and without makers' marks. No. 284 is possibly 17th century. The tiny examples are perhaps toys.

277. Circumferential upper and basal plain bands, flat crown, D18.51mm H16.73mm. PAS SUSS-129C73. *East Sussex.*

278. A basal deep rim, pointed crown, D13.5mm H11mm. *South East Dorset.*

279. Cast pewter, a circumferential basal plain band with one groove, one ridge and a rim; repeating engraved concentric circles on the sides, an erratic right-hand spiral of punched circular pits on the crown, a longitudinal mould line each side, D15.09mm H14.81mm. UKDFD 40763. *Buckinghamshire.*

280. Cast pewter, slightly distorted, a circumferential basal hatched band with one groove; a shallow rim, concentric circles of punched small circular pits on the sides and large on the crown, D20mm H22mm. *Wiltshire.*

281. Ten concentric grooves with shallow ridges between on the sides, rows of punched circular pits on the crown, D16mm H18.5mm. *East Devon.*

282. Nine concentric grooves with ridges between on the sides, rows of punched circular pits on the crown, D17mm H20mm. *East Devon.*

283. Possibly hybridised; composite two piece sheet copper-alloy; the body is (?) hammered, (?) die-punched or (?) deep drawn, while the flat crown is separately soldered; a circumferential basal plain band with one groove and a rim, concentric circles of possibly punched circular pits on the sides, the upper rim of which curves outwards, the crown has die-punched lozenge-shaped pits within a partial border of punched small circular pits; D22mm H15mm. UKDFD 40344. *Wiltshire.*

284. Silver, either cast or hammered sheet, hexagonal footprint, carinated sides, punched square pits on the sides, embossed flowers on the crown configured six around one, D14.5mm H12mm. *South Wales.*

285. A circumferential basal plain band with two grooves, curlicues simulating foliate on the sides, bands of punched circular pits on the crown, D13.8mm H14mm. *South Devon.*

286. A circumferential basal plain band with four grooves and a pronounced rim, hatching between the upper two grooves; curlicues simulating foliate on the sides surmounted by a band of hatching, lines of punched circular pits on the crown, D15mm H16.6mm. *South East Dorset.*

287. A circumferential basal plain band with a rim and a band of hatching; linear and curvilinear simulating foliate on the sides and surmounted by a band of hatching, lines of punched circular pits on the crown, D18mm H20mm. *South Somerset.*

288. A circumferential basal plain band with two obliquely hatched bands and a rim, curlicues simulating foliate on the sides, a tonsured crown with a nipple surrounded by irregularly configured punched circular pits and gouge marks, D17.4mm H17.4mm. *South East Dorset.*

289. Steel crown, gilded sides, a circumferential basal band embossed with cross-hatching, scissors, (?) pin cushion, needle-threader and a bottle; lozenge-shaped pits on the sides and five concentric circles of die-punched circular pits the crown, D13.8mm H15mm. *South West Wiltshire.*

290. A circumferential basal band with five grooves, three ridges and a rim; embossed with a bird, key, scissors, geometric and organic motifs and an open book; circular pits on the sides and die-punched concentric circles of circular pits on the crown, D14.5mm H17.4mm. PAS LON-3DE715. *River Thames foreshore, London.*

291. Hammered or deep drawn sheet silver, the basal half of the sides has five bands, two plain, the upper with a makers mark – G C, a lower band of a repeating chevrons, a wide band of curlicues and chevrons, and an upper band of repeating crescents; lozenge-shaped pits on the sides with a dividing band of chevrons and six concentric circles of die-punched square/circular pits on the crown, D17mm H17mm. *East Devon.*

Domed thimbles 18th – early 19th century

All are probably English. Unless specified otherwise, deep drawn sheet silver with mechanically knurled circular pits on the sides and die-stamped circular pits on the crown; circumferential engraved grooves on the sides creating bands, either plain or with engraved and punched decoration.

292. Four circumferential grooves creating three bands and a rim, repeating chevrons in the lowest band, repeating foliate on a field of vertical zigzags in the central band, and an upper band of repeating chevrons; a right-hand spiral of punched circular pits on the sides and concentric circles on the crown, D14mm H22mm. *South Devon.*

293. A flat crown, two circumferential grooves in the basal half of the sides, below the basal groove is a band of repeating chevrons above which is a band of punched repeating geometric rectilinear and another two bands of repeating chevrons; the crown has punched concentric circles of circular pits within two concentric circles, D15mm H22mm. *South Devon.*

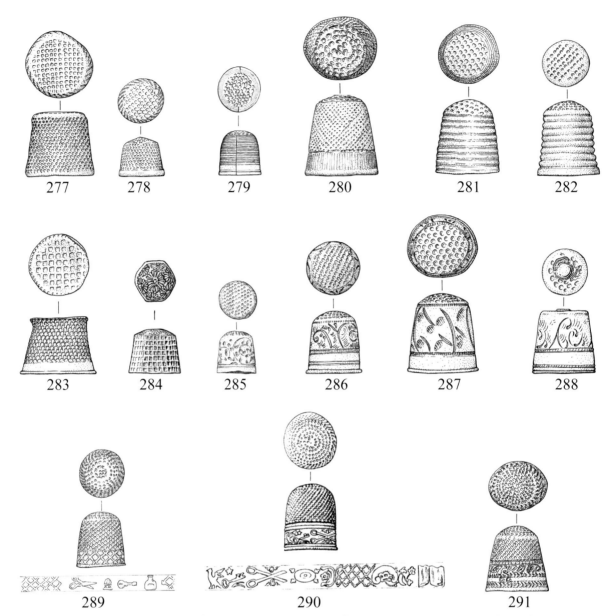

277   278   279   280   281   282

283   284   285   286   287   288

289   290   291

294. Four circumferential engraved grooves in the basal half of the sides, the upper and basal two of which are hatched; the central band has repeating dashes forming two-strand interlace and a voided shield-shaped cartouche; the crown has a plain band and four concentric circles of punched circular pits up to a tonsure, and a small hole pierced by a needle, D15mm H25.2mm. *Staffordshire.*

295. Composite three-piece, steel cap lost, longitudinal scarfed and lapped and horizontal butt soldered seams, a circumferential plain band covers the abraded basal half of the sides with vestiges of upper and basal voided bands of zigzags or repeating chevrons or triangles, D16.3mm H22mm. *South Devon.*

296. Steel cap lost; a circumferential plain band with four grooves and two ridges in the basal half of the sides, D11mm H13.6mm. *South West Wiltshire.*

297. Steel cap lost, a circumferential plain band with ten circumferential grooves in the basal half of the sides, D18.5mm H24mm. *South Devon.*

298. Rust on the crown is remains of a steel cap, a circumferential plain band with two grooves and two bands of repeating ring-and-dot motifs in the lower two thirds of the sides; D12.5mm H15mm. *North Dorset.*

299. Steel cap lost; the lower two-thirds of the sides has five partial circumferential bands – alternate lozenges and flower-like motifs with either side repeating vertical dashes; and vertical curvilinear bands forming a cartouche engraved with the owner's initials F.C, D14mm H20mm. *South West Wiltshire.*

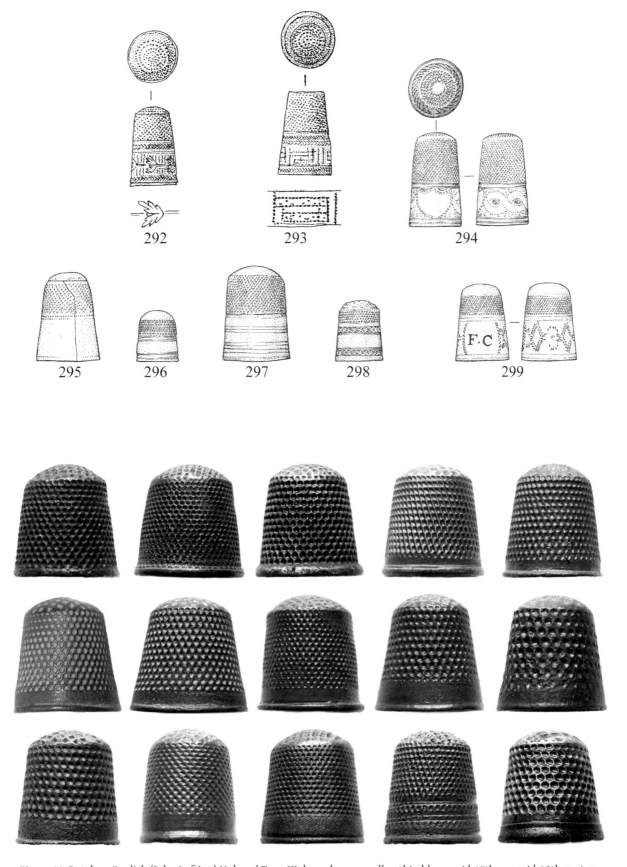

Figure 33. Dutch or English (John Lofting) Holmes' Type III domed copper-alloy thimbles *c.* mid-17th – *c.* mid-18th century.

Figure 34. Miscellaneous domed copper-alloy, pewter and silver thimbles *c.* mid 18th – *c.* mid-19th century.
(*one is perhaps 17th century)

Metal Open-Top Thimbles

Open-top thimbles *c.*14th – *c.*15th century

From a secure *c.* early 14th-century deposit in London's River Thames foreshore, Mudlarks excavated two copper-alloy thimbles of a type apparently unrecorded from other British depositions (Nos 300-301). Each is distinctive by being tall with a large circular aperture in its relatively pointed crown (after Mills 1999, Nos NM.60-61). Whether these thimbles are cast or sheet with longitudinal soldered seams is unclear though cast is probable. Cf ill. 3 in Langedijk and Boon 1999 for a *c.*14th – *c.*15th century sheet copper-alloy specimen found in Rakin, a major street in Amsterdam: it has a rounded crown and a longitudinal soldered butt seam, one side is punched or drilled with circular pits

Figure 35. Open-top copper-alloy thimbles *c.*14th century. After Mills 1999, NM.60, NM.61.

forming a shield-shaped coat of arms within a multi-cusped cartouche, columns of similar pits cover the rest of the sides. Isbister 2002 records another, excavated in a *c.*14th- – *c.*15th-century context near Perm in Russia; and a further two in Feldhaus 1931, 245a are now in Altes Museum, Berlin.

Isbister 2002 suggests these thimbles are a Russian evolvement that progressed from Mongolia during the 13th-century expansion of the Golden Horde, while others say 15th- – 16th-century Nuremberg is their place of origin. The datable evidence from London and Amsterdam supports the Golden Horde theory. Curiously, neither Holmes 1985 nor McConnel 1991 *et al* mention this type of thimble.

From Britain several much squatter probably cast specimens are known, each with a similar large circular aperture in its rounded crown, two of which are included here (Nos 302-303). Their closet equivalent seems to be a Hispano-Moresque cast copper-alloy open-top thimble (Isbister 2002) but whether the ones found in Britain originated in Spain or even North Africa is uncertain.

Open-top thimbles *c.*14th century

Uncertain provenance. All are copper alloy, probably cast, featuring a large circular aperture in the crown apex. Unless specified otherwise, undecorated and with circumferential plain bands and engraved grooves, with punched circular pits in columns.

300. The bare crown tapers sharply and has two circumferential grooves, upper and basal plain bands, basal with one groove; pits in columns though the drawing suggests a right-hand spiral, D *c.*28mm H *c.*25mm. After Mills 1999. *River Thames foreshore, London.*

301. The bare crown tapers sharply and has two circumferential grooves, upper and basal plain bands, basal with one groove; columns of pits on half of the sides, the other half has an organic pattern of punched pits forming a multi-petalled flower, dimensions unknown. After Mills 1999. *River Thames foreshore, London.*

302. Basal rim slightly ragged, circumferential upper and basal plain bands, each with one groove; pits in columns, several oblique; D16.5mm H16.5mm. *Isle of Wight.*

303. Pits in concentric circles; D17mm H19mm. *South Somerset.*

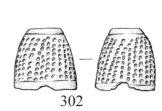
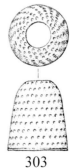

300   301   302   303

Metal Finger-Guards

Finger-guards *c.* early 18th – *c.* mid-19th century

A finger-guard – aka finger-protector, finger-shield – fits on the first finger of the opposite hand used to hold the needle and protects that finger from the needle point. Like thimbles, finger-guards would have been in everyday use but, paradoxically, excavated examples, either by archaeologists or detectorists, appear to be uncommon in Britain. Three types made from metal are apparent: Ring-type (No. 304), Domed (Nos 305-307), and Open-top: none of the latter were noted during this present study.

Ring-type finger-guards date from around the early 18th century until about the mid-19th and were manufactured in France, Russia, England, the Netherlands and the USA from sheet metal, either gold, silver or silver-gilt, and, to a lesser extent, copper alloy (Holmes 1985). Narrow hoops with a central butt seam, either soldered or unsoldered, and large integral oval or ovoid bezels, makes them resemble finger-rings, hence their name 'Ring-type'. Unsoldered seams would facilitate use with different size fingers. Bezels engraved or die-punched with repeating transverse grooves and ridges were popular, and this same ornamentation may continue along both sections of the hoops (No. 304). Also known is other engraved decoration, as is enamel and semi-precious stones. American examples confirmed as found in Britain are absent from this present assemblage.

Circa 19th-century English-made domed finger-guards may be deep-drawn sheet silver or copper alloy though in the latter metal are rarely seen. They look like domed thimbles with a section cut out from the crown down to as much as two thirds of the sides. A basal folded-back rim is normal though separate soldered rims are known. Although many are plain, die-punched or engraved decoration such as concentric grooves and ridges or ornate foliate is typical (Nos 305-307).

Open-top finger-guards, invariably deep-drawn sheet silver, are also *c.*19th-century English, and easily confused with earlier composite two-piece thimbles with lost crowns. If a longitudinal soldered seam is visible, then it is probably a thimble and not a finger-guard.

Ring-type finger-guards *c.* early 18th – *c.* mid-19th century

Possibly English. Sheet silver with an unsoldered butt seam and engraved decoration.

304. Repeating transverse deep grooves and ridges on an ovoid bezel and a similar groove and ridges around the hoop; hoop D16.5mm, bezel L24.5mm W14.5mm. UKDFD 4036. *Essex.*

Domed finger-guards *c.*19th century

All are possibly English. Deep-drawn sheet silver; unless specified otherwise, one-piece with basal engraved decoration while upper sides and crowns are plain.

305. A pronounced folded-back rim, four concentric basal grooves and ridges, the aperture has a bifurcate lower edge, D18mm H24.5mm. *Dorset.*

306. A pronounced folded-back rim, above the rim are three circumferential bands – repeating shield-shapes, cross-hatching, repeating shield-shapes and a groove, D17mm H21.8mm. *Dorset.*

307. A separate soldered pronounced faceted rim, above the rim is one groove and a band of zigzags, cross-hatching and annulets; remainder of the sides have repeating concentric grooves and ridges, D18mm H22mm. *South Devon.*

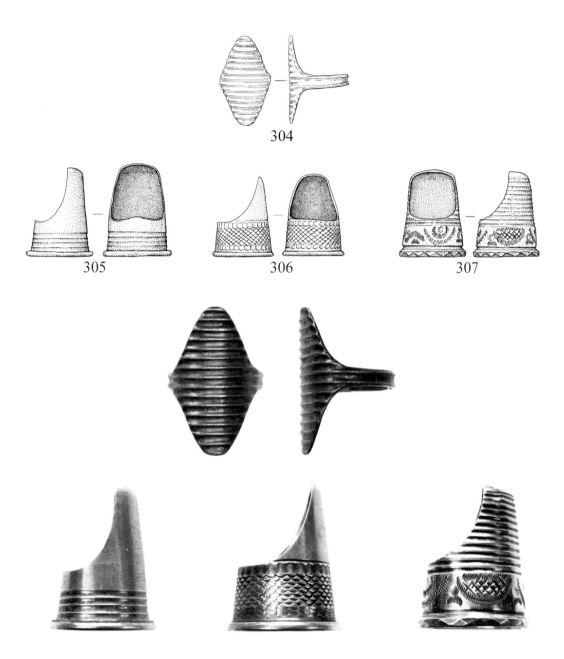

Figure 36. Ring-type and domed silver finger-guards *c*.18th – *c*.19th century.

Metal Palm-Irons

Palm-irons *c.*17th – *c.*20th century

Despite the present writer having recorded 17 examples (10 catalogued herein) of these substantial cast copper-alloy or malleable cast-iron or steel circular tools with lugs (aka 'ears' in a *c.*1900 catalogue), named sailmakers' or sailors' palm-irons (aka plates or palm-guard pushers), until early March 2012 precisely how they were used was an enigma. Why they are called 'irons' is perhaps due to the later forms being made of iron or steel; therefore we can infer that copper-alloy examples are possibly earlier. Apart from PAS database SUSS-864CD1, LON-43E204, LON-E2C8A5, SWYOR-438A46, DEV-0ACE07; and Fig. 184, No. 191 in *Excavations in Southwark 1973-76 & Lambeth 1973-79 MoL & Joint Pub. No. 3 LAMAS SAS* (Mark Brown's Wharf), palm-irons seem unrecorded in Britain by archaeology. Furthermore, they appear to be absent in the respective collections of several national and international maritime museums. The National Maritime Museum at Greenwich possesses an anonymous French artist's album of pen and ink drawings depicting sailmakers' tools, one of which appears to be a Read Type (see below) IIb or IIc metal palm-iron with waisted, roughly globular lugs, shown both detached and affixed to a sailmaker's leather palm (*Dictionnaire de la Marine a Voiles et a Vapeu* 1847; facsimile, 1980. Rene Baudouin, acc. PA12128). Moreover, Juan José Navarro's *Álbum del Marqués de la Victoria's 1719-1756* also depicts a Read Type II palm-iron with three equidistant semicircular pierced lugs attached to a palm: whether this palm is leather or canvas is unclear as is the attachment method of the iron to the palm (Fig. 37). The date of this publication perhaps suggests that lugged palm-irons were current in at least the late 17th century. Paradoxically, a trawl of the abundance of metal material culture recovered from 17th-, 18th- and 19th-century shipwrecks around Australia revealed the absence of metal palm-irons of any type.

Possibly the earliest record of a sailmaker's palm fitted with an iron without lugs is a sketch by Swedish author Ake Classon Ralamb in his *Skeps Byggerij* 1691 (Pawson 2010 & 2018, see below). There is other evidence that certain sailmakers' or sailors' palm-irons without lugs, made from cast copper-alloy, malleable cast-iron, steel or even organic material, date to at least the late 17th century and indeed are still produced and used today, and in the very recent past, aluminium too (Pawson 2010 & 2018). Palm-irons of any type were and still are affixed to an extensive range of different styles of leather or canvas palms (Pawson 2010 & 2018). Essentially, a palm fits over a hand, with an iron inset into the palm near the ball of the thumb, and made in both right- and left-handed versions (Fig. 39). Sailors' palms are generally of lighter construction than those used by sailmakers (Pawson 2010 & 2018). Perhaps the earliest surviving possible leather palm came from the 1545 wreck of the *Mary Rose*; apparently found in association with a horn disc, perhaps a palm-iron, which is now lost (a drawing of the palm shows no marks suggesting a disc being sewn to the leather). Pawson provides evidence for leather palm makers' in Britain, America and mainland Europe, and are respectively known as 'British Style', 'Dutch Style', 'French Style', 'Hamburg Style' and 'Portugese Style'. Sailmakers' leather palms with metal irons were also used in the leather trade, though to a lesser extent than specialised iron 'collar palms' and 'plier-palms' (Salaman 1986, Figs 9:5, 9:6, 9:10, 9.11 and pp 260).

Purely by chance, the present writer established contact with the aforesaid Des Pawson MBE at his Museum of Knots and Sailor's Ropework, Ipswich; he is a long-time researcher into sailmakers' palm-irons, other maritime tools and ropes and knots, too. Pawson is rightly considered an international authority on these subjects and has written and published ten monographs – Monograph #8 *Sailmakers' Palms* 2010 (revised and expanded 2018), with his kind permission, is the one considered here. Although Pawson's research provides solid evidence of palm-irons with lugs being used in the 18th, 19th and 20th centuries, by how much they antecede the former is unclear. Notwithstanding, some lugged palm-irons

76

described here are credited to Mudlarks who excavated them from reliable 17th-century contexts in the River Thames foreshore, London. The aforesaid archaeological example from Mark Brown's Wharf, London came from a 1680-1710 stratified context, a deposition compatible with the Thames recoveries. Others here are detecting finds from inland rural depositions. As many windmills used canvas sails, which would have required regular repair or replacement, it provides a plausible explanation for some of the latter recoveries (pers. comm. Des Pawson). Interestingly, the only surviving unearthed malleable iron or steel palm-irons in the known record, and included here, are from the River Thames foreshore, London, preserved by the anaerobic conditions. Malleable iron or steel examples are unrecorded from inland sites so far, where they ought to be; corrosion and metal-detector ferrous discrimination presumably prevents their discovery, or they are found and simply not recognised.

For stitching – called seaming – the varying weights of canvas and sailcloth used for sails, hatch-tarpaulins, boat-covers and a variety of other shipboard purposes, the steel needles employed by sailmakers or sailors are straight and triangular-section. Steel needles for stitching up sacks or packs and, until recent years, darning fire brigade canvas delivery-hose, are shallow triangular cross-section with upturned points. Stitching ropes along the edges of canvas sails, awnings and weather cloths – called roping – requires heavier-gauge needles, and palm-irons necessarily had or have larger pits. On any type of palm-iron, pits act the same as those on a thimble and help prevent the eye-end of the needle from slipping. Whatever the sewing task, especially roping, considerable pressure is needed to push the needle through canvas, which without the aid of a metal palm-iron would cause serious injury to the user's palm. Twine is used in sewing, several strands of which are threaded through the needle eye, formed into a bight and twisted together, and then smoothed by drawing through a block of beeswax that helps waterproof and preserved the twine, and makes it easier to draw through canvas.

Six types and six sub-types of metal palm-iron are now confidently recognised. The present writer's previous Typology, published in the *Finds Research Group AD 700-1700 Datasheet 45* Post-Medieval Palm-irons, 2013; and in *The Searcher* February 2010 and October 2012, is revised as below.

Type I: circular, flat, without rims or lugs.
Type II: circular, flat, with rims and three equidistant peripheral pierced lugs.
Sub-type IIa: circular, concave with domed reverse and three equidistant peripheral pierced lugs.
Sub-type IIb: circular, flat, with rims and three equidistant peripheral unpierced lugs.
Sub-type IIc: circular, concave with domed reverse and three equidistant peripheral unpierced lugs.
Type III: circular, flat, with rims and four equidistant peripheral pierced lugs.
Sub-type IIIa: circular, flat, with rims and four equidistant peripheral unpierced lugs.
Type IV: circular, wedge-shaped, without rims or lugs.
Sub-type IVa: circular, wedge-shaped, with rims without lugs.
Sub-type IVb: circular, wedge-shaped, with rims and three equidistant peripheral unpierced lugs.
Type V: hexagonal, wedge-shaped, without lugs.
Type VI: circular, flat, with rims and three equidistant pairs of attachment-holes in the rim.

Recovered by Dutch marine archaeologists from a merchant vessel (name unknown) wrecked *c.*1658 in the Wadden Sea off North Holland, the Netherlands, is the only recorded Type VI cast copper-alloy palm-iron. It is circular, flat, with a rim and three pairs of probably drilled attachment-holes (Fig. 37); cf Nederlandse Archeologische Rapporten 041, Amersfoort 2012 Objectnummer [MA]BZN8-338, Burgzand Noord 8 / BZN8 / Lelie 1.

Type V hexagonal wedge-shaped malleable iron or steel palm-irons without lugs were made by Ike Manchester Senior, probably for himself, in New Bedford, United States of America, (1885-1960)

(Pawson 2010 & 2018) though none are recorded as found in Britain. Rectangular palm-irons with four lugs may also have existed, though this is speculative (Pawson 2010 & 2018). Three other circular flat possibilities are known: one in Otley Museum, Yorkshire has (?) moulded oval pits and a single pierced lug (Pawson 2010 & 2018), a scalloped edge curiosity with circular pits and a central (?) rivet-hole found near Wolverhampton (Fig. 40); and a 1500 25 French jetton with punched circular pits and three (?) attachment-holes (Egan 2005, No. 969). The latter, from a stratified c.1500-50 archaeological context in London, suggests reuse as a palm-iron, which if correct may mean that metal palm-irons were in use back at least to the 16th century. Coins adapted as palm-irons, is another plausible possibility (Pawson 2010 & 2018), and No. 308 is perhaps an 18th-19th century halfpenny reused as a palm-iron. The aforesaid 11th- – 15th-century *acutrudia*, Middle Eastern and Turkish cast copper-alloy palm pushers, apparently were not used with leather or canvas palms.

Lugs may be semicircular (Nos 309-314), roughly globular (Nos 315-318) or triangular cross-section (No. 322): the latter two shapes may also be waisted (Nos 315-316, 318, 322). Typical on irons having semicircular lugs is a single attachment-hole piercing all lugs from front to back. These holes are circular or subcircular, the former suggesting drilling and the latter perhaps moulding, sloppy drilling or wear. On those irons with roughly globular or triangular cross-section lugs discussed here, apart from No. 317, which is anomalous by having one of its lugs pierced transversely from side to side (? drilled), the lugs are unpierced. Type I irons may have been used without any form of palm though inset into leather palms is a possibility. Lugged irons of any type were attached to palms either with twine stitching, using wires (No. 322) or riveting (No. 314), whereas wedge-shaped irons without lugs were or are secured by angled rawhide (Nos 319-321 & Fig. 39).

Two palm-irons with pierced semicircular lugs and one without lugs, all from secure c.17th- – c.18th-century deposits in the River Thames foreshore, London, are described as 'Early Sailors' Palms' by Holmes in *Thimbles Notes and Queries No. 18* 1993. Holmes provides evidence in the same Note for palm-irons with pierced semicircular lugs and without lugs being made by R Timmins and Sons, a Birmingham firm of toolmakers active between c.1791 - c.1889. An engraving of four palm-irons, one lacking lugs and three with pierced semicircular lugs, produced by this firm, is depicted in Plate No. 66 in Kenneth D Roberts Pattern Book *Tools for the Trades and Crafts* 1976. This book was first printed c.1845, however, the engravings may date to c.1820 or earlier. Interestingly, roughly globular lugs, pierced or otherwise, are absent from the Pattern Book, therefore whether R Timmins and Sons produced palm-irons of this type is uncertain. For reasons unclear, to date, Type II palm-irons are more common than Type I from rural depositions in Southern England, including the River Thames foreshore, London. The only Type IV, Sub-type IVa and Sub-type IVb palm-irons recorded during this present study came from the Thames foreshore, London; and Type III and Sub-type IIIa palm-irons with four lugs were not noted. For the latter see Pawson 2010 pp 10, 14-16, 27, 44 and Pawson 2018 pp 10, 14-17, 79.

A frontal panel of pits is characteristic on all of the aforesaid types of palm-iron. Pits on known Type I palm-irons are circular and on Type II and IIa either circular or lozenge-shaped, and, seemingly uncommonly, rectangular, triangular or pentagonal – none of the latter three shapes were noted during this present study; the only known Type VI palm-iron has elongated oval pits configured in three concentric circles. Examination of the available palm-irons or depicted by Pawson indicates that circular pits appear mainly drilled, though moulded is a probability on others. Circular pits are configured in concentric circles, bands, random or a mixture. Engraved concentric circles, probably used for aligning the pits, are evident in the recess of No. 317.

Of the palm-irons (and possible palm-iron) illustrated and discussed here, Nos 308-311, 313, 316-317, 319-321 have circular pits while on No. 312 they are shallow and irregular-shaped, perhaps indicating poor drilling, wear, or inferior casting. The pits of Nos 310, 312, 314 are gouged, probably caused by needles slipping. The crudeness of some palm-irons suggests they were cast from moulds impressed with old used irons (pers. comm. Des Pawson). Nos 314-315, 318, 322 have lozenge-shaped pits. Three palm-irons (Nos 311, 313, 315) have pierced pits, probably worn through by extensive usage, which on No. 311 are blocked with rust that also stains the recess, possibly remnants of steel needles broken off.

Read Type I palm-irons

Possibly a reused British copper halfpenny, circular, flat, with drilled pits, without rims or lugs, *c*.18th- – *c*.19th-century.

308. Irregular configuration of pits on the front, one pit on the reverse, D28.3mm T1.2mm. *Staffordshire*.

Read Type II palm-irons

Provenance uncertain. Cast copper-alloy, circular, flat, with rims, three equidistant peripheral pierced lugs, and; unless specified otherwise, drilled pits, *c*.17th – *c*.19th century.

309. Much-abraded front panel, pits configured four within a circle, D25mm T6.8mm. *Wiltshire*.

310. One lug broken, much abraded front panel showing probable needle gouges, pits possibly in concentric circles, D44mm T7mm. *North Devon*.

311. One lug broken off, four concentric circles of pits; two pits pierced, both retaining rust, presumably remnants of steel needles; D37mm T5mm. *East Devon*.

Read Sub-type IIa palm-irons

Provenance uncertain. Cast copper-alloy, circular; concave front and domed reverse, with rims, three equidistant peripheral pierced lugs; and unless specified otherwise, drilled pits, *c*.17th – *c*.19th century.

312. Front panel is much abraded and shows probable needle gouges, pits possibly in concentric circles or random, D43mm T8mm. *River Thames foreshore, London*.

313. Most of the rim is worn away and the front panel is partially abraded, pits in concentric circles, central pit pierced, D28.5mm T3mm. *East Devon*.

314. Front panel has moulded lozenge-shaped pits and shows a probable needle gouge, each lug retains a separate copper-alloy rivet and rove, D42mm T7.72mm. PAS SWYOR-438A46. *North Yorkshire*.

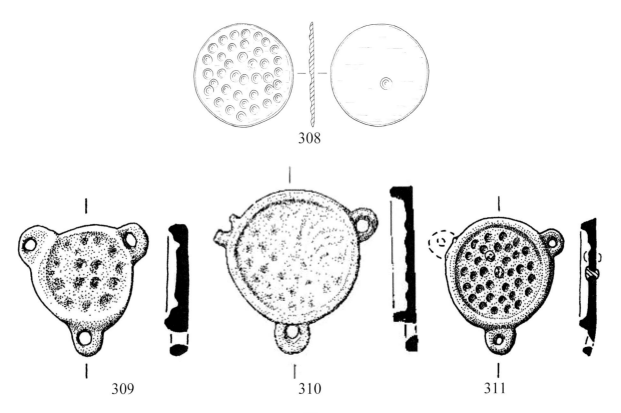

308

309   310   311

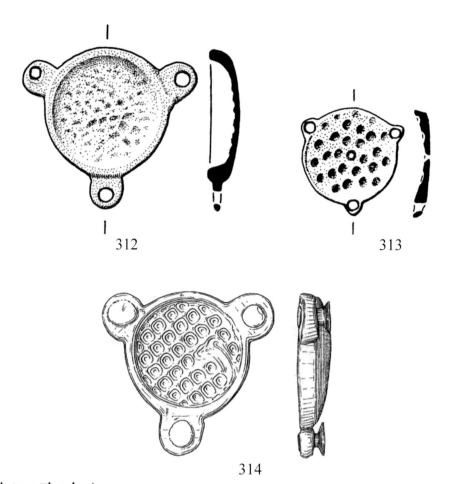

312   313

314

Read Sub-type IIb palm-irons

Provenance uncertain. Circular, flat; unless specified otherwise, cast copper alloy; with drilled pits, rims and three equidistant peripheral unpierced lugs; *c*.17th – *c*.19th century.

315. Moulded lozenge-shaped pits, several small holes probably caused by needles, D35.9mm T5mm. PAS SUSS-864CD1. *East Sussex.*

316. Malleable iron or steel, probable bands of moulded pits, D38.5mm T5mm. *River Thames foreshore, London.*

317. Pits in two concentric circles and a central cross of five pits; three engraved concentric circles, probably for aligning the pits; one lug is pierced therefore this palm-iron is anomalous, D36.4mm T5mm. *East Devon.*

Read Sub-type IIc palm-irons

Provenance uncertain. Malleable iron or steel, circular, concave front and domed reverse, moulded lozenge-shaped pits, three equidistant peripheral waisted, unpierced lugs, *c*.17th – *c*.19th century.

318. D33mm T6.7mm. *River Thames foreshore, London.*

Read Type III palm-irons

Probably British. Malleable iron or steel, circular, wedge-shaped, drilled or moulded pits, without rims or lugs, 20th century.

319. A circle of six pits and one central large pit, D20mm T18mm. *Via Des Pawson.*

320. Recessed reverse, two concentric circles of large pits and one central large pit, D23mm T18mm. *Via Des Pawson.*

Read Sub-type IIIa palm-irons

British. Malleable iron or steel, circular, wedge-shaped, with rims without lugs, drilled or moulded pits; 20th century.

321. Recessed reverse with the maker's name W H SMITH & SON REDDITCH around illegible lettering, two concentric circles of pits and one central pit, D20mm T18mm. *Via Des Pawson.*

Read Sub-type IIIb palm-irons

Provenance uncertain. Malleable iron or steel, circular, wedge-shaped, with rims and three equidistant peripheral unpierced lugs, *c.*20th century.

322. Recessed reverse, moulded lozenge-shaped pits, a length of copper-alloy circular cross-section wire is secured around two triangular cross-section lugs, D37mm T21mm. *River Thames foreshore, London.*

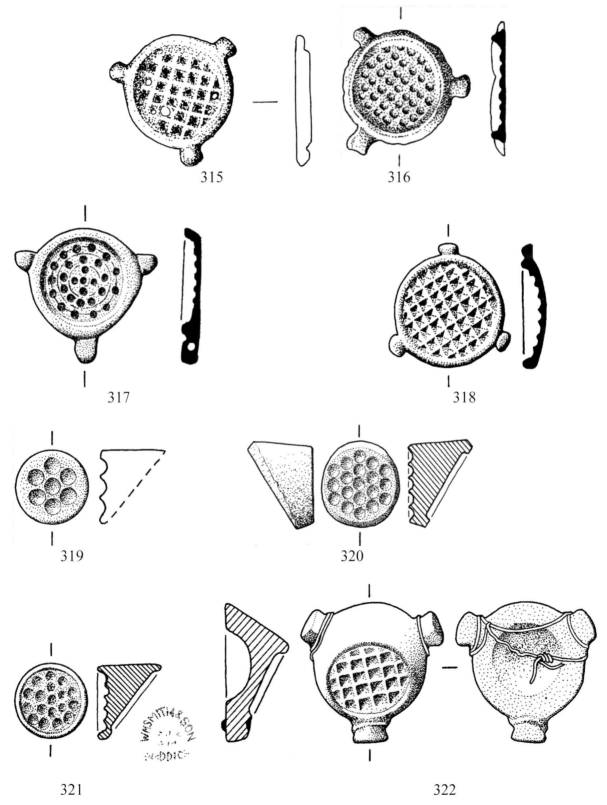

Figure 37. Read Type V cast copper-alloy palm-iron, from the *c.*1658 *Wadden Sea shipwreck*. Photo reproduced courtesy of the Rijksdienst voor Cultureel Erfgoed.

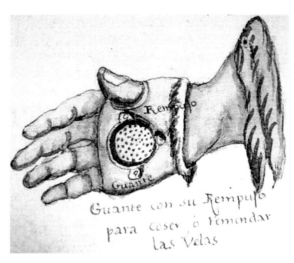

Figure 38. Sketch of a sailmaker's palm fitted with a Read Type II palm-iron in *Álbum del Marqués de la Victoria 1719-56*. After Pawson 2010 pp 11.

Figure 39. Sailmaker's leather palm 19th century. Note angled section of rawhide and inset metal probable Read Type III wedge-shaped iron. Photo copyright © and reproduced courtesy of Penlee House Gallery and Museum, Penzance.

Figure 40. Copper-alloy and malleable iron or steel palm-irons and copper-alloy possible palm-iron *c.*17th – *c.*20th century. Some photos copyright © and reproduced courtesy of the PAS.

Metal So-called Palm Guards

Leaden so-called palm-guards *c*. late post-medieval

It is convenient here to discuss the ubiquitous cast lead or lead/tin alloy so-called 'palm-guards', known in varying sizes of roughly elliptical or circular – usually described as shaped like shells of Swan Mussels or Oysters or spoon-shaped – flat one side and convex the other (Fig. 41). There is not any evidence to confirm that halves of Swan Mussel shells acted as casting moulds for these leaden objects. The convex sides of examples similar to Swan Mussels – also other shapes – frequently feature one or more discoidal impressions, often claimed as caused by adductor muscle scars present on shell interiors (Fig. 41). Although many do resemble the general shape of Swan Mussels, the position of such impressions generally does not mirror the correct positions of anterior and posterior adductor muscle scars. Only a single scar exists on the inside of one half of a shell, therefore multiple impressions cannot be from a Swan Mussel. Precisely what these impressions represent is unclear.

Logically, the convex side cupped into the palm of the hand, implying the flat side pushed the metal needle, the head of which would have marked the soft metal. Although possible metal needle marks are noted on some, there is not any evidence to confirm their use as palm-irons in any maritime environment or land-based agricultural, leather or textile industry.

A frequently expounded explanation why these leaden objects come to light so often in the rural environment is they are palm-irons (see below) used when stitching-closed hessian sacks holding grain or wool, however, polished wooden, not metal, needles were the traditional and preferred tool for this task. To penetrate hessian, wooden needles did not require great pressure, which perhaps negates such a theory. The Walsall Leather Museum has no knowledge of these leaden objects and they are absent from Salaman's *Dictionary of Leather-working Tools 1700-1950*, 1986. The Museum of English Rural Life has one, acc. 95/1, described as a 'leather-worker's palm guard' and with a dubious provenance – '… found in a piece of agricultural land along with military uniform buttons and copper coins dating from the 18th and 19th centuries'. In the absence of irrefutable proof, we can only speculate on the true purpose of these common objects: regarding their age, late post-medieval is likely.

The PAS database has two leaden objects considered as possible palm-guards, each attached through a hole in an oyster shell – IOW-A9A877 and SUR-BF7905 – and another recorded as a possible palm-guard – UKDFD 10488 – bears an impression of a 19th-century coastguard button. None show possible needle marks and all seem unrelated to the leaden objects discussed here.

Figure 41. Leaden so-called palm-guards, possibly *c*. late post-medieval, *Yorkshire, County Durham, Lincolnshire* and *Yorkshire*. Note none, one or two circular impressions in convex sides and absence of confirmed needle marks on either side. Photos copyright © and reproduced courtesy of the PAS.

Bibliography

Bax A and Martin C J M. 1974. 'De Liefde. A Dutch East Indiaman lost on the Out Skerries, Shetland in 1711', *International Journal of Nautical Archaeology and Underwater Exploration, vol. 3, pp 81-90*. London. Semina Press.

Beaudry, C M. 2006. *Finding the Material Culture of Needlework and Sewing*. New Haven USA. Yale University Press.

Blake, W and Green J. 1986. A Mid-XVI-Century Portuguese Wreck in the Seychelles. *International Journal of Nautical Archaeology and Underwater Exploration vol.15.1: pp 1-23*. London. Academic Press.

Bonnefoux, E P M and Paris F E. 1847. *Dictionnaire de la Marine a Voiles et a Vapeu*. Facsimile, 1980. Rene Baudouin. Paris.

Bonwick G J. 1964. *Seamanship Handbook Basic Studies*. London. The Maritime Press.

Burn, D P. 1993. *Identifying Steel-Cored Thimbles*. Dorset Thimble Society.

Burn, D P. 2001. Early Thimbles. *Thimble Collectors International.*

Cuming, H S. 1879. On Thimbles. *Journal of the British Archaeological Association pp 238-242.*

Daniels, D. 2012. *John Lofting*. Published privately.

Davidson, G R. 1952. *Corinth. vol 12, The Minor Objects*. Princeton. Princeton University Press.

De Mello, U P. 1979. The Shipwreck of the galleon *Sacramento*-1668 off Brazil. *International Journal of Nautical Archaeology and Underwater Exploration, 8.3: pp 211-23*. London. Semina Press.

De Smet, A. 1992. *De Vingerhoed in Het Kunstambacht*. Vercruysse, Belgium.

Doorman, G. 16th - 18th century. *Octroolen voor Uitvindingen in de Nederlanden uit de 16e-18e eeuw*. Netherlands Search Room Nationaal Archief S11 A 54A.

Egan, G. 1998. *The Medieval Household Daily Living c.1150-c.1450*. Medieval Finds from Excavations in London: 6. MoL.

Egan, G. 2005. *Material Culture in London in an Age of Transition, Tudor and Stuart Period Finds c1450 - c1700 from Excavations at Riverside Sites in Southwark*. MoLAS monograph 19.

Eigmüller M and Inge L. 2014. *Nürnberger Fingerhüte*. Museum I22I20I18I Kühnertsgasse. Nuremberg.

Fairclough, K R. 2004. Lofting, John c.1659-1742. *Oxford Dictionary of National Biography*. Oxford University Press. Oxford.

Falconer, W. 1769. *An Universal Dictionary of the Marine*. London.

Feldhaus, F M. 1931. *Die technic der antike und des mittelalters*. Akademische verlagsgesellschaft Athenaion. Wildpark, Potsdam.

Gardener J and Allen, M J (eds). 2005. *Before the Mast Life and Death Aboard the 'Mary Rose' - Archaeology of the 'Mary Rose' S V4*. Portsmouth. The Mary Rose Trust.

Greif, H. 1984. *Talks about Thimbles: A Cultural Historical Study*. Fingerhutmuseum Creglingen, Klagenfurt. Austria.

Greif, H. 1986. *Nuremberg Thimble-makers*. Thimble Collectors International.

Griffiths, D; Philpott R A and Egan, G. 2007. *Meols: the Archaeology of the North Wirral Coast: Discoveries and Observations in the 19th and 20th Centuries*. Oxford University School of Archaeology. Monograph 68. School of Archaeology, Oxford.

Groves, S. 1966. *The History of Needlework Tools and Accessories*. London. Country Life Books.

Hill, E. 1995. Thimbles and Thimble Rings from the circum-Caribbean Region, 1500-1800: Chronology and Identification. *Historical Archaeology 1995, vol 29(1): pp 84-92*. New Mexico.

Hinton, D (ed.) 1988. Excavations in Southwark 1973-76 and Lambeth 1973-79, London. MoL, Joint Pub. No. 3 LAMAS and SAS.

Holmes, E F. 1985. *A History of Thimbles*. USA. Rosemont Publishing and Printing Corporation.

Holmes, E F. 1986. Nautical Archaeology. *Thimble Collector's International Bulletin,* July 2-5.

Holmes, E F. 1987. Early Brass Thimbles. *Thimble Collector's International Bulletin,* July: 3-11.

Holmes, E F. 1988. Thimbles. Finds Research Group AD 700-1700, *Datasheet 9.*

Holmes, E F. 1990. 6:2. *Thimbles Notes and Queries.* London. The Thimble Society.

Holmes, E F. 1990. 8:2. *Thimbles Notes and Queries.* London. The Thimble Society.

Holmes, E F. 1993. Early Sailors' Palms in *Thimbles Notes and Queries No. 18.* London. The Thimble Society.

Holthuizen, H. 1984. *Working Thimbles in Amsterdam, 1550-1700. De Vingerhoed,* June: pp 13-15. Amstelveen.

Houghton, J. 1727/28. *A Collection of Letters for Improvement of Husbandry and Trade, Rev. ed. Vol.* (letter 14 dated 13 March. 1683). London.

Isbister, M and W. 2014. *The role of religious belief in the determination of the shape of English silver thimbles in the mid 17th century.* Moosbach.

Isbister, M and W. 2014. *Old Thimbles.* Moosbach.

Isbister, M and W. 2015. *More About Thimbles vol. 1.* Moosbach.

Isbister, M and W. 2015. *More About Thimbles vol. 2.* Moosbach.

Isbister, M and W. 2015. *16th and 17th century European 'keepsake' thimbles.* Moosbach.

Isbister, M and W. 2016. *More About Thimbles vol. 3.* Moosbach.

Isbister, M and W. 2017. *More About Thimbles vol. 4.* Moosbach.

Isbister, W. 2015. *The Anatomy of the Thimble.* Moosbach.

Kyriacou C, Mee F and Rogers N (eds). 2004. *Treasures of York.* York. York Archaeological Trust.

Landauer, M. Late 16th century. *Landauer Foundation Memorial Book.* Nuremberg.

Langedijke C and Boon F. 1999. *Vinerhoeden en naairingen uit de Amsterdamse boden: Prductietechnieken vanaf De Late Middeleeuwen,* Archeologische Werkgemeenschap voor Nederlands, Reeks 2. Amsterdam. Bartels.

Larn R, McBride P and Davis R. 1974. The mid-17th century merchant ship found near Mullion Cove, Cornwall. Second interim report. *International Journal of Nautical Archaeology and Underwater Exploration, 3.1: pp 67- 79.*

Margeson, S. 1993. *Norwich Households: The Medieval and Post-Medieval Finds from Norwich Survey Excavations 1971-1978.* East Anglian Archaeology Report No. 58.

Martin, C [J M]. 1998a. *Scotland's Historic Shipwrecks.* London. Page(s): 113 Held at RCAHMS E.5.14.MAR.

McConnel, B. 1991. *The Letts Guide to Collecting Thimbles.* London. Charles Letts and Co Ltd.

Mendel, K. *c.*1425/6-. *Mendelschen Institute Housebook.* Nuremberg.

Mileusnic, Z (ed.). 2004. *The Venetian Shipwreck at Gnalić.* Annales Mediterranea. Biograd Na Moru. Croatia. Koper.

Mills, N. 1999. *Medieval Artefacts.* London. Greenlight Publishing.

Moore, J J. 1801. *British Mariner's Vocabulary.* London. Hurst.

National Maritime Museum, Greenwich. *Undated album of sailmakers' tools by an anonymous French Artist.* acc. PA12128.

Navarro, J J. 1719-56. *Álbum Del Marqués De La Victoria.* Cadiz. Facsimile, 1995, Lunwerg Editores. Madrid.

Nederlandse Archeologische Rapporten 041, Objectnummer [MA]BZN8-338. Burgzand Noord 8 / BZN8 / Lelie 1. 2012. Amersfoort.

Pawson, D. 2010. *Sailmakers' Palms.* Ipswich. Museum of Sailors' Knots and Ropework.

Pawson, D. 2018. *Sailmakers' Palms expanded ed.* Ipswich. Museum of Sailors' Knots and Ropes.

Price R and Muckelroy K. 1977. The *Kennemerland* site, The third and fourth seasons 1974 and 1976. An interim report. *International Journal of Nautical Archaeology and Underwater Exploration, 6.3:* pp 167-218.

Ralamb, A C. 1691. *Skeps Byggerij eller adelig ofnings tionde tom.* Facimile, 1943, Sjohistoriska Museet, Malmo.

Read, B A. 1988. *History Beneath Our Feet.* Braunton. Merlin Books Ltd.

Read, B A. 1995. *History Beneath Our Feet* 2nd ed. Ipswich. Anglia Publishing.

Read, B A. February 2010. Post-Medieval Palm-Guard Pushers in *The Searcher,* pp 48-9. Searcher Publications.

Read, B A. October 2012. Post-Medieval Palm-irons in *The Searcher,* pp 33-35. Searcher Publications.

Read, B A. September 2013. *Datasheet 45: Post-Medieval Palm-irons.* Finds Research Group AD 700-1700.

Register of 16th - 18th-century Patents for Inventions. The Netherlands National Archive.

Ridley, G. 1992. *Dive Scotland: The Northern Isles and East Coast,* Revision London Page(s): 186-7, No. 2391.

Roberts, K D. 1976. *Tools for the Trades and Crafts.* Fitzwilliam NH, USA. Ken Roberts Publishing Company.

Sachsen, H. 1568. *Eigentliche Beschreibung aller Stände auff Erden.* Frankfurt and Mayn.

Salaman, R A. 1986. *Dictionary of Leather-working Tools 1700-1950.* London. George Allen and Unwin.

Schuster, J. 2014. *A Medieval Sewing-Thimble From Dolbenmaen, Gwynedd.* Templecombe.

Steel, D. 1794. *The Elements and Practice of Rigging and Seamanship,* 2 vols. London.

Thompson, A; Grew, F and Schofield, J. 1984. Excavations at Aldgate, 1974. *Post-Medieval Archaeology 18* pp 1-148.

Timmins, Richard and Sons. 1994. *The Victorian Catalogue of Tools for Trades and Crafts.* Intro' by Philip Walker Facsimile of Trade Catalogue *c.*1845. London. Studio Editions.

Trentmann, F. 2012. *The Oxford Handbook of the History of Consumption.* Oxford University Press. Oxford.

Weigel, C. 1698. *Abbildung der Germain-Nützlichen Haupt-Stände.* Nuremberg.

Whittaker, I G. 1998. *Off Scotland: A Comprehensive Record of Maritime and Aviation Losses in Scottish Waters.* pp 35 held at RCAHMS E.5.14.WHI. Edinburgh.

Wilson, R J A. 2016. On Early Thimbles: A Seventh-Century-AD Example from Punta Secca, Sicily, in Context. *Oxford Journal of Archaeology, 35: 413-43, Issue 4.* Oxford.

Woodfield, C. 1981. Finds from the Free Grammar School at the Whitefriars, Coventry, ca. 1545-1557-58. *Post-Medieval Archaeology 15*: pp 81-159.